CEO LIFELINES

CEO LIFELINES

*Nine Commitments Every
Leader Must Make*

S ALVATORE D . F AZZOLARI

OPEN BOOK
EDITIONS
A Berrett–Koehler Partner

CEO LIFELINES
Nine Commitments Every Leader Must Make

iUniverse books may be ordered through booksellers or by contacting:

iUniverse
1663 Liberty Drive
Bloomington, IN 47403
www.iuniverse.com
1-800-Authors (1-800-288-4677)

ISBN: 978-1-4917-2578-8 (sc)
ISBN: 978-1-4917-2577-1 (hc)
ISBN: 978-1-4917-2579-5 (e)

Library of Congress Control Number: 2014903131

Printed in the United States of America.

iUniverse rev. date: 04/07/2014

CONTENTS

Preface. ix

Acknowledgments. xiii

Introduction. xv

Part 1: The Three Practices for Sustained Leadership

Chapter 1   Precocious Characteristics 3

Chapter 2   Indispensable Experiences 23

Chapter 3   Proactive Actions. 39

Part 2: The Six Practices of a Healthy Enterprise

Chapter 4   Business Model. 65

Chapter 5   Learning Entity. 77

Chapter 6   Exceptional Capabilities 109

Chapter 7   People Excellence 131

Chapter 8   Distinctive Culture. 145

Chapter 9   Core Philosophy. 157

Part 3: The Serendipity of Chance, Good and Bad

Chapter 10   Luck—The Wild Card of a CEO's Success. 169

Chapter 11   Summary and Action Tools 181

Final Remarks 207

Appendix 1: Climb the Summit—Harsco's Journey 209

Appendix 2: The Power of Luck—My Journey 221

Notes. 227

About the Author 235

Index 237

PREFACE

If your actions inspire others to dream more, learn more,
do more and become more, you are a leader.
—John Quincy Adams[1]

Sometimes our most significant personal and career insights are waiting to be discovered *right in front of us*. As I thought about writing this book and considered organizational themes, it occurred to me just how important lifelines are in the construction business. A lifeline device consists of a length of high-strength synthetic rope that is securely fixed to a heavy-duty steel clip. Workers attach these lifelines to the superstructure so they can safely do their work while perched dozens of stories above the ground.

For more than three decades, I climbed Harsco Corporation's steel superstructures at construction sites all around the world. I initially made these potentially dangerous climbs as a newly hired auditor, but eventually I scaled these buildings as the company's CFO and finally as president, CEO, and chairman.

So it's no wonder that lifelines emerged as the principle organizing metaphor for this book and that the safety devices came to represent the enduring characteristics I believe organizational leaders, at every level, must possess to ensure the success of the employees they lead and the enterprise they serve.

Not a Memoir

Although this book is not a memoir, you'll find references to my personal leadership journey throughout. I include these details because they illustrate how a leader can use his precocious characteristics—indispensable experiences and penchant toward taking proactive actions—to succeed.

I believe my personal story has a great deal to do with the success I enjoyed as a leader. I immigrated to this country with my poor but proud Italian family and began my career as an entry-level auditor without political or family connections. Yet I was able to rise to the position of chairman, president, and chief executive officer of a $3 billion company. In many ways, I am the embodiment of what is described as "living the American Dream."

I was successful because I worked hard, but what really pulled me up the ladder rungs of success were the lifelines handed to me along the way by other generous leaders. Because of that good fortune, I tried to mirror the generosity of those leaders who helped me throughout my career and always offered a bit of the same luck of association to the rising talented leaders I supported, coached, and mentored along the way.

Mountaineering Metaphor

I also use mountaineering metaphors throughout the book to capture the essence of the challenges leaders face in today's tumultuous and competitive global marketplace. Just as the construction industry relies on lifelines to ensure safety, mountaineers rely on a similar clip-and-rope assembly called a *belay* to prevent falls as they climb. Like the construction industry lifeline, the belay is a useful narrative device that further illustrates the individual and organizational challenges all leaders face.

My Qualifications

This book is derived from almost four decades of professional experience, a lifetime of learning, and careful studies of exceptional companies.

During my professional career, I was fortunate to obtain a broad base of indispensable experiences working in a multitude of industries, principally those that provide products and services to the steel, nonresidential construction, rail, energy, and defense industries. In addition, my board work exposed me to other industries like coatings, specialty chemicals, building products, and global-engineering services. I also have experience in academia and government services from which to draw the conclusions offered in this book. I have a broad and diversified background, having held such positions as auditor, senior auditor, director of internal audit, corporate controller, treasurer, chief financial officer, president, chief executive officer, chairman, and board director. I also have experience as a management consultant, author, speaker, and entrepreneur.

I hold professional certifications as a certified public accountant (inactive) and a certified information-systems auditor (inactive). I am a Pennsylvania State University alumni fellow and was awarded the distinguished 2012 Business Achievement Award by Beta Gamma Sigma. I had the privilege and honor to attend three separate "Good to Great" dialogue sessions with Jim Collins at his lab in Boulder, Colorado.

Final Word about My Personal Journey

I truly believe that something good always comes from a bad experience. Sadly, my period of leadership as chairman, president, and CEO of Harsco ended in February 2012 after fifty months of leading the company through the most challenging period in its history. Our key end-markets were materially and adversely affected by two extreme global economic shocks. As a direct result of these events, we saw plunging revenues (a 25 percent decline) and pricing pressures weigh heavily on the performance of the company.

In addition to navigating unprecedented economic turbulence, Harsco simultaneously began executing a necessary business-transformation strategy centered mainly on *globalization, innovation,* and *optimization.* Transformations, by their nature, are complex and usually take many years to complete successfully.

These facts alone demonstrate that a meaningful and measurable amount of work was successfully completed by my team under the most severe economic conditions in the modern history of the company. (For more details on the Harsco story, see appendix 1 in this book, "Climb the Summit—Harsco's Journey.") Notwithstanding this fact, in the fifth year of that vital transformation, the Harsco board decided it was best to bring in a new set of eyes to complete the process, so we amicably separated.

Perhaps I shouldn't have been surprised. The average tenure of a Fortune 500 CEO is fifty-four months. And nearly 80 percent of S&P 500 CEOs depart their companies before retirement. This trend will likely continue because of ongoing volatility and uncertainty throughout the world.

As CEOs, we must always remember that we are accountable for what happens regardless of the circumstances or the economic environment. The ultimate responsibility always resides with the CEO. It's a real no-excuse job!

The Good and the Lucky

Despite circumstances that forced me to leave a job I loved, I have much to be grateful for, and I still believe in luck. I am grateful for the lifeline that my predecessor handed me by believing in me throughout my career and pulling me up to the summit position of CEO. He took an early interest in my professional growth and made it a priority to share his accumulated experience and teach whenever new issues presented the opportunity. Without those indispensable experiences, this book would not have been possible. In this and many other ways, I have been a lucky leader indeed!

If reading this book makes you a better, more productive, more capable, more engaged and effective leader, then I will count this as further success—and a lifeline and even luck we share together.

ACKNOWLEDGMENTS

There is no better expression of appreciation than a sincere and heartfelt thank-you. So I want to thank everyone who helped me create this book. I am fortunate to have such a loving family and so many loyal and supportive friends. You are all true lifelines!

A special thank-you goes to my extraordinary editor, Mark Morrow, who made a significant contribution to this book. His counsel, creativity, and guidance were instrumental in bringing my story to life. I am honored and humbled that he devoted countless hours to this project, and I am deeply indebted.

Thank you to the early believers who provided invaluable insight and focus and were important contributors to shaping the book, including my good friend Sage Newman; professor Richard A. D'Aveni of the Tuck School of Business at Dartmouth; my son Michael Fazzolari; and the talented author John Kador. I am most grateful for their intuition and counsel as the book evolved from a series of unrelated chapters to a cohesive and fully integrated story of how nine lifelines and luck can shape your business career and the health of an enterprise. Without their wisdom, guidance, and creativity, this book would not have been possible. Also contributing early to the framing of the book were my loving, supportive wife, Karen Fazzolari, and our oldest son, Salvatore V. Fazzolari. I owe a tremendous amount of gratitude to both of you.

I would like to especially thank the author and business-management guru Jim Collins. Without his permission to use material from his exceptional books and his inspiration over the years, this book would not have been possible.

Others who made a notable contribution to this book and to whom I owe gratitude include Paul Coppock, Caesar Sweitzer, Stephen Schnoor, Pradeep Anand, Joseph Viviano, Frank C. Sullivan, Jim Demitrieus, Christopher Marcocci, Rita Marcocci, Maria Hamilton, Michael Murchie, Michael Pavone, Nicodemo Fazzolari, Sean Sullivan, and Drake Nicholas, Esq. In addition, Dr. Jay Lemons, president of Susquehanna University, and the great Penn State Harrisburg team of Dr. Mukund Kulkarni, Dr. Stephen Schappe, Dr. Richard Young, and Marissa Hoover. Thank you for your sage advice. It was invaluable in crystallizing and focusing the material that resulted in this book.

INTRODUCTION

Great things are done by a series of small things brought together.
—Vincent Van Gogh[2]

CEO Lifelines: Nine Commitments Every Leader Must Make is a book that requires its readers to have an adventuresome spirit and a willingness to engage in meaningful self-evaluation. It's a book that promises to take its readers on a journey to discover the essential characteristics that underpin strong, decisive leadership and build enduring, high-performance organizations. I believe leaders willing to implement and live the nine lifelines (or practices) outlined here will be fully prepared for the inevitable global shocks that will test both their leadership mettle and the strength of the organizations they lead. Readers should use this book as a road map to avoid potential career and organizational turbulence, and as a resource for appropriate antidotes and countermeasures to keep moving forward even in the worst of times.

How This Book Is Organized: Three Key Parts

The nine leadership practices you'll read about in this book highlight the lifelines that directly impact a leader's career and the enterprise he or she leads. I use metaphors to describe the journey I believe these extraordinary leaders must make. One of the principal organizing metaphors, mountaineering, seems particularly suited to describing this journey, so you will see its use throughout the book.

In addition to the mountaineering metaphors, I have divided the book into three lifeline segments focusing on personal, enterprise, and luck.

» *Part 1: The Three Practices for Sustained Leadership.* Part 1 covers three personal lifelines that encourage personal growth and improved individual performance. Leaders willing to enthusiastically embrace these important personal lifelines should be able to endure any economic environment. This section includes a lifelines inventory and assessment of these practices so that readers can accurately identify areas of improvement.

» *Part 2: The Six Practices of a Healthy Enterprise.* Leaders who vigorously implement the enterprise lifelines outlined in part 2 should see sustained improvement in their organizations' operating results while simultaneously building an enduring company with the potential to last for generations no matter the economic circumstances. The six practices are interdependent and equally important. These lifelines are also necessary countermeasures to unforeseen disasters (chance events), such as a worldwide economic downturn brought on by national or geopolitical events. These essential lifelines serve as an antidote to the impact of potential misfortunes. This section includes an enterprise lifelines inventory and assessment of practices that will help your organization assess its readiness.

» *Part 3: The Serendipity of Chance, Good and Bad.* Part 3 of the book covers the often-ignored element of luck, the wild card of a CEO's success. I have coined the term *luck spread* to describe this element of success and failure. Both individual leaders and companies need to understand the power of luck and how the luck spread can dramatically alter an assumed path to the summit of success. It's also important to acknowledge that the luck spread's nature is that good luck is sometimes mistaken for skill, strong leadership, and exceptional performance, while bad luck is often mistaken for inadequate skill, bad management, and poor performance. Which side of the luck spread a leader ultimately lands on is largely out of his or her control, but I believe the best countermeasure to a negative luck spread is implementing the nine essential lifelines outlined in this book.

Some of the nine leadership lifelines are included because they support and encourage employee growth and improved individual performance. Other lifelines are the specific leadership characteristics that drive a commitment to improved operational performance and the desire to build a successful enterprise that endures for generations.

The nine personal and enterprise lifelines (three personal and six enterprise) represent the distillation of what I've learned about leading organizations and individual employees. The personal lifelines demonstrate

» a keen understanding of the thirty key precocious-leadership characteristics,

» an ability to learn through indispensable experiences,

» a fearless and proactive approach to the job, while the enterprise lifelines encourage

» a tenacious focus on an innovative business model,

» an ability to learn from success and failure,

» an exceptional focus on operational capabilities,

» a focus on building and maintaining an A-team,

» a passion for creating a high-functioning culture, and

» an ability to articulate and live by a shared philosophy.

All three personal and six enterprise lifelines explored in this book are interdependent and important for the success of a leader and his or her organization. Moreover, I believe these nine lifelines offer a strong framework that can propel both individual leaders and their organizations toward excellence.

Value of These Lifelines

You may say on first look that these nine lifelines are not very groundbreaking. However, I urge you to have the heart to look beneath the surface. It is there that I believe you will discover your own trusted lifeline and a basis of support as you journey toward becoming a new breed of exceptional manager. As a leader, I worked extraordinarily hard to offer the lifelines discussed in this book to every employee and organization I served. If you believe you are an equally committed leader and you're looking for a lifeline to secure your leadership position, then I invite you to *clip on* to this book and use it to securely build a leadership success story.

The figure below shows how the nine lifelines fit together to form an integrated framework that promotes both personal and enterprise excellence. It also shows that luck is a factor that must be considered in building the nine lifelines.

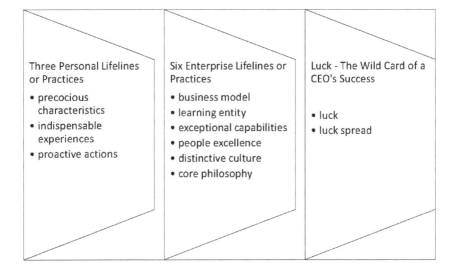

Three Personal Lifelines or Practices

- precocious characteristics
- indispensable experiences
- proactive actions

Six Enterprise Lifelines or Practices

- business model
- learning entity
- exceptional capabilities
- people excellence
- distinctive culture
- core philosophy

Luck - The Wild Card of a CEO's Success

- luck
- luck spread

Mountaineering Metaphors

Metaphors are powerful mechanisms for a writer to connect with readers. I use mountaineering metaphors throughout the book to convey and capture the essence of the nine leadership lifelines. It is an effective lens for the reader to see the arduous journey that individuals and organizations face today in navigating a tumultuous global economic environment. (Mountaineering is a component of Alpinism, which is the broad appreciation of mountain regions.)

Here are two of the key mountaineering metaphors used in the book:

» *Hope for the best, but plan for the worst.* In an article for the Brattle Group, George Oldfield, Michael Cragg, and Jehan deFonseka used this paraphrase from the book *Deadly Summit* to explain the US credit crisis. In its newsletter, the group noted that a leader must clearly understand that it is always positive to be hopeful, but it is also imperative to prepare for the worst as a hedge against that potential outcome.[3] I believe that leaders who aggressively and skillfully implement the nine leadership lifelines in this book will effectively implement that recommendation.

» *Getting up the mountain is optional, getting down the mountain is mandatory.* Every business leader and company must clearly understand that it is possible to become trapped in the so-called "Death Zone." In the book *The Climb: Tragic Ambitions on Everest*, authors Anatoli Boukreev and G. Weston DeWalt define the Death Zone as "any elevation above 8,000 meters where extended exposure to subzero temperatures and oxygen deprivation combine and kill, quickly."[4]

The Death Zone in business can be a severe global shock like the Great Recession or a significant and precipitous drop in orders due to a disruptive new technology. Mountaineers and true leaders must be well prepared for the journey and ensure that enough personal and organizational strength and resources exist to get safely down the mountain, if necessary.

Climbing Code

Mountaineering also includes a Climbing Code, and I have adapted this code for my purposes in this book because I believe that the underlying philosophy fits well with the central metaphor of lifelines I outline in this book. In particular, I used the book *Mountaineering: The Freedom of the*

Hills, edited by Ronald C. Eng, for my inspiration.[5] Here are two relevant rules that apply to both the individual and organizational concepts used in *CEO Lifelines*:

> » *Never climb beyond your ability and knowledge.* Individual leaders and their organizations must recognize that beginning a climb without the right skills and exceptional capabilities will make the journey difficult at best and perhaps even lethal.

> » *Never let judgment be overruled by a desire to reach the summit when choosing a route or deciding whether to turn back.* Leaders often let their emotions and personal ambitions cloud their judgment. This can have serious negative consequences, especially when a career or an organization is in a precarious predicament.

General Comments about the Book

This book is focused on the nine lifelines I have observed, lived, and implemented on a global scale. It is intended to be a practical guide and workbook that includes related tools for building careers and organizations. Consequently, the book is focused mostly on professionals, business leaders, newly appointed CEOs with no prior CEO experience, CEOs of private or family-owned companies, and leaders of nonprofit organizations. If you are responsible for leading a small sales team or a business unit or even a large enterprise, this lifeline is for you.

Moreover, this book is intended to be a lifeline for MBA and undergraduate business students. I believe this book offers students a real-life perspective on the challenges of becoming a business leader in today's highly complex and increasingly turbulent economic environment.

My hope is that readers of this book will develop a precocious ability to recognize and accept the critical lifelines they're offered during their ascent toward career and organizational success.

PART 1

The Three Practices for Sustained Leadership

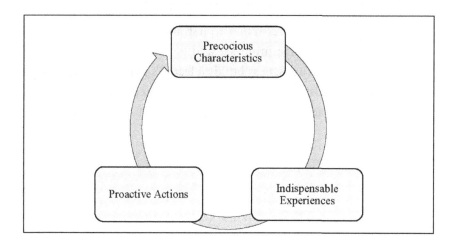

Part 1 provides a framework for personal growth and success as a leader. It is a personal guide and workbook for leaders to follow in building vital lifelines that are necessary to climb the summit. Here is a summary of each chapter:

» *Chapter 1: Precocious Characteristics.* Leaders must possess thirty critical characteristics in order to succeed as leaders and move their organizations forward. Some are innate and others must be developed, but leadership strength and suitability are defined by these characteristics.

Throughout my career, I have been fascinated by successful leaders and wanted to better understand what characteristics made these individuals so special. Thus, for almost four decades, I have been cataloguing characteristics that I believed distinguished these talented leaders from everyone else. The thirty characteristics outlined in this chapter are the culmination of my work.

» *Chapter 2: Indispensable Experiences.* Leaders, like everyone else, are defined by their experiences. CEOs must be better than most at gathering up the right collection of essential experiences and skills to face the challenge and enormity of the job.

» *Chapter 3: Proactive Actions.* First and foremost, leaders must possess a proactive mind-set and be fearless in the execution of their job. Fearlessness builds a leader's personal courage and provides indispensable job experiences. There are a multitude of specific proactive actions that leaders must take in order to be successful.

CHAPTER 1

Precocious Characteristics

We should take care not to make the intellect our god.
It has, of course, powerful muscles, but no personality.
—Albert Einstein[6]

Imagine being a climb leader en route to the summit. The safety of your party is dependent on you making many right decisions along the way, relying on what I call your *precocious characteristics*. So what are those special qualities that a leader must possess to be successful? According to *Mountaineering: The Freedom of the Hills*, edited by Ronald C. Eng, they include:

> judgment, common sense, mountain sense, navigation, teaching, coaching, training, anticipation, guardian (team and environment), survival, planning, building (team), learning, initiator and arbitrator.[7]

It's no different in the business world. In order to successfully lead their respective teams on the ascent to the summit, both mountaineers and business leaders must possess vital precocious characteristics. As we will explore in this chapter, the same characteristics that make an elite mountaineer can also be found in a great business leader. The parallels are striking, but business leaders need a more expansive skill set due to the immense requirements of the job.

A New Breed of Business Leader

Business leaders today are confronted with tremendous challenges. In addition to global turbulence and an extremely competitive landscape, CEOs and other leaders face a highly burdensome regulatory environment, increasingly independent boards, and ever more vocal shareholders. With growing volatility and uncertainty, particularly as the pace of globalization and technological change accelerates, attracting and retaining exceptional talent is more important than ever.

Clearly, a new breed of professional leader is required for the reset global economy. This chapter outlines thirty precocious characteristics that business leaders need to possess and provides specific arguments about why each is important. Many of these characteristics are innate, while others can be developed with the right character-building experiences, ongoing training, and a focused commitment to build them. All leaders are defined by the strength, depth, and quality of these characteristics. Moreover, it is these characteristics that ultimately determine the success of a leader and the organization he or she leads. Here's the list:

1. Integrity
2. Instincts
3. Perspective
4. Discipline
5. Wisdom
6. Willingness to apologize
7. Loyalty
8. Navigational skills
9. Optimism and passion

10. Good execution

11. Humility

12. Communication skills

13. Ability to be proactive

14. Transparency

15. Inquisitiveness

16. Truthfulness

17. Courage

18. Cost mind-set

19. Ability to build an enduring enterprise

20. Generative thinking

21. Continuous self-improvement

22. Equanimity

23. Negotiating skills

24. Gratefulness

25. Giving nature

26. Team-building talents

27. Accountability

28. Perseverance

29. Survival instincts

30. Learning, teaching, and coaching ability

Let's look at each of these in more detail.

1. Integrity

Leaders must possess uncompromising integrity. It is a characteristic that is the backbone of an ethical culture. Integrity does not need much definition because ethical and unethical behavior is usually easy to recognize, but for the record, integrity means a leader

» does the right things, for the right reasons, in the right way;

» fully complies not only with the letter of the law but with the spirit of the law;

» follows all regulations and policies and codes of conduct;

» conducts business honestly and ethically; and

» respects and maintains confidentiality.

Integrity above all defines a leader and must be manifested in his or her every action. Extraordinary leaders and organizations are always built on a foundation of uncompromising integrity and ethical business practices.

Example: Uncompromising Integrity

One of the best examples of business integrity that I have come across is in Walter Isaacson's extraordinary book *Steve Jobs*. Isaacson recounts the story of Stephen Wozniak, Apple's cofounder, and how he and Jobs developed their first computer. Wozniak was compelled by his strong ethics to offer the machine to Hewlett-Packard because he designed the computer while working there. He believed it was the ethical thing to do. Of course he was right. He demonstrated the machine to HP managers, they declined, and the rest is history.

---

2. Instincts

All exceptional leaders possess a natural ability to use their instincts or intuition. The author Agatha Christie captured the essence of instinct extremely well when she said, "Instinct is a marvelous thing. It can neither be explained nor ignored."[8] A powerful example of this leadership trait is Apple's Steve Jobs, who built a world-changing organization pretty much on the strength of his extraordinary instinct and intuition.

3. Perspective

Perspective can only be developed through vital experiences, a lifetime of learning, and the development of the precocious characteristics outlined in this chapter. Without these critical background elements, it is difficult to develop a sound perspective. In fact, boards of directors exist because these individuals have developed invaluable perspective over many decades of experience.

John Sununu, former governor of New Hampshire, had this to say about the topic: "Perspective gives us the ability to accurately contrast the large with the small, the important with the less important. Without it we are lost in a world where all ideas, news, and information look the same. We cannot differentiate, we cannot prioritize, and we cannot make good choices."[9]

Innovative leader Steve Jobs characterized perspective at Apple in this way: "A lot of people in our industry haven't had very diverse experiences. So they don't have enough dots to connect, and they end up with very linear solutions without a broad perspective on the problem. The broader one's understanding is of the human experience, the better design we will have."[10]

Never shortchange or underestimate the importance of perspective. Lack of it is almost always a serious error for a leader.

4. Discipline

Extraordinary leaders are disciplined and consistent in what they think, do, and say, and they are not easily distracted from their focus. They adhere to a code of conduct that includes commitment to continuous self-improvement and a strong work ethic. Disciplined leaders pay attention to the most-important mission-critical matters, such as customers, employees, their leadership team, assessing risk, setting strategy, and establishing the tone for the organization. Clara Barton, the founder of the American Red Cross, captured the substance of discipline when she said, "The surest test of discipline is its absence."[11]

5. Wisdom

Wise leaders consistently demonstrate sound judgment, quality thinking, and common sense. Gifted leaders know how to blend insight with analytical skills to solve problems and inspire an organization through effective and timely decision making. President Herbert Hoover once said, "Wisdom consists not so much in knowing what to do in the ultimate as knowing what to do next."[12]

6. Willingness to Apologize

Outstanding leaders have the courage, integrity, and humility to apologize when it's appropriate and necessary. This is an integral part of a framework of leadership accountability and responsibility. The author John Kador captures this point well in his book *Effective Apology: Mending Fences, Building Bridges, and Restoring Trust*:

> The capacity of leaders to apologize can determine their ability to create the kinds of high-trust organizations required to navigate challenging times … Today, apology is increasingly regarded as an expression of strength, character, and integrity … Apology is a critical skill of our time … Many leaders hate to apologize, offering elaborate defenses instead of accepting responsibility for mistakes … Apology is an attitude as well as a practice. It's a marker of confident leadership.[13]

I'll share a personal example. In 2010, when the construction markets evaporated and Harsco's overall business was materially and adversely impacted, we struggled with our scenario analysis due to unprecedented volatility and uncertainty. As a consequence, we had to lower our earnings guidance during the course of the year. Later that year, I took an opportunity to apologize at an investor conference during one-on-one meetings with major shareholders. My apology was simple, direct, and well received. This is what I said:

I apologize for the earnings guidance revisions. As the CEO, I understand that I am completely accountable and responsible. I take full responsibility for what has happened and I am sorry.

In addition to the apology, it is important for leaders to clearly explain steps taken to move the organization forward or provide assurances that the mistake is a valuable lesson learned and it will not be repeated.

7. Loyalty

Talented leaders have a unique ability to command unconditional loyalty and unwavering respect from their teams. They inspire people in the organization through integrity, hard work, vision, and engagement. These leaders create a superior execution culture that demands exceptional performance and inspires full commitment to the cause. This faithful adherence to the leader does not mean blindly following every word or every command. On the contrary, it means that the leader's integrity, ethical practices, personal character, humility, and other precocious characteristics have earned the team's respect, trust, and loyalty. The author Mark Twain captured the point in a humorous but effective way when he said, "Loyalty to the country always. Loyalty to the government when it deserves it."[14]

8. Navigational Skills

Here's what the authors Mark Houston and Kathy Cosley had to say about navigating your way around risks in the book *Alpine Climbing: Techniques to Take You Higher*: "Many risks change throughout the day. It is important to anticipate these changes and track them as you climb, watching the weather, your energy level, the clock, and changes in snow and ice conditions as the day warms. Think ahead to your descent route."[15]

Capable leaders are adept at navigating through periods of instability and uncertainty. Leaders must be able to successfully steer their organizations through global shocks, and they must be able to anticipate the unexpected. In today's highly tempestuous economic environment, this characteristic is essential. Leaders must always project a sense of calm and total control no matter the circumstances.

Over the past fifteen years, we have seen with some frequency unforeseen events, such as the Asian financial crisis, the dot-com bubble, the 9/11 terrorist attack on the United States, the US financial crisis, the Arab Spring, the European sovereign debt crisis, and the tsunami that caused the 2011 nuclear meltdown at the Fukushima power plant in Japan. Events like these are essentially impossible to predict, but as any Alpine climber knows, anticipating and preparing for potential risks is key to survival. Leaders must be equally careful about managing risks to ensure that potentially catastrophic events do not adversely impact their organizations.

9. Optimism and Passion

Incredible leaders consistently manifest optimism and passion. The many daunting challenges of today's highly tumultuous and complex global business environment require that leaders have an unwavering faith in their survival. Strong leaders also have a deep passion and an infectious enthusiasm for the organization, and they show it by working tirelessly and being fully engaged in the execution of their strategy. This optimism and passion is manifested (just as it is for Alpine climbers) by their extraordinary resilience, focus under stress, and equanimity, as evidenced by the way they work relentlessly to keep their team together.

The best example of a world leader with infectious optimism was President Ronald Reagan. He was passionate and truly an eternal optimist. Here's something Reagan said that captures the essence of his optimism: "Every new day begins with possibilities. It's up to us to fill it with the things that move us toward progress and peace."[16]

10. Good Execution

Gifted leaders consistently deliver on their commitments. They do not make promises that they can't keep. They don't overpromise or underpromise. They have an unshakeable faith in their ability to deliver results and create an organizational culture of execution. Good leaders understand that without consistent execution, their organizations have little chance of reaching the summit.

11. Humility

Leaders today must be humble and self-aware, especially in team-oriented organizations where individual hubris is an absolute roadblock to productive collaboration. The novelist C. S. Lewis captured the essence of humility when he said, "Humility is not thinking less of yourself, it's thinking of yourself less."[17]

12. Communication Skills

Leaders must also be outstanding communicators and be able to articulate a clear, consistent, and easily understood strategy that resonates at all levels of the organization. President Ronald Reagan was known as the Great Communicator. Former US Senator Fred Thompson captured Reagan's communication abilities when he said that "it boils down to three basic traits: he was simple; he was clear; he was sincere."[18] All leaders should keep these three traits in mind as they develop and implement their communication strategy.

13. Ability to Be Proactive

Accomplished leaders are proactive, not reactive, and they easily adapt to change. As with professional mountaineers, anticipating change is a crucial survival skill. As Houston and Cosley point out, climbers must anticipate "every change in terrain, route difficulty, or hazard [that] may require a new strategy, mode of movement, or protective system to deal with new circumstances."[19] Leaders must be equally proactive and vigilant to recognize that change is occurring and act appropriately.

14. Transparency

Transparency is a hallmark of any good leader. Leaders operate in an open and transparent way with the board of directors, shareholders, customers, suppliers, employees, and the community. They create an environment with a strong code of conduct. And they operate within a framework of openness, integrity, accountability, and responsibility.

15. Inquisitiveness

Skilled leaders have an inquisitive mind. They are always asking questions and not assuming or taking anything for granted. These leaders have the ability to connect the dots—that is, they have the capacity to anticipate. In fact, this ability to see things that others can't or refuse to see is one of the most important qualities of a new-age leader.

16. Truthfulness

Capable leaders create a truthful culture in which everyone in the organization is comfortable with candid and open dialogue and all employees feel empowered to speak with impunity. The retribution-free climate is essential for a healthy culture and is one of the keys to creating a learning-focused environment for an organization. The author Mark Twain captured the true meaning of this important characteristic when he said, "Truth is the most valuable thing we have. Let us economize it."[20]

17. Courage

Superb leaders consistently manifest courage by standing up for deeply held beliefs and insisting that others on their team display the same accountability. These courageous leaders also take blame when things go wrong and easily give praise for the success of others. Courage also means that the leader balances both the short-term needs and the long-term health of the organization.

Here is an example from my experience as CEO of Harsco. As our key markets contracted, we continued to build critical lifelines at Harsco while enduring the company's most significant downturn in modern history. These investments included building new capabilities, such as global shared services, a global supply chain, and a Lean continuous-improvement discipline. We also continued our investment in people, innovation, and expansion into emerging markets. We were steadfast in our resolve to improve the enterprise for the long-term.

Here's another example, from a September 2012 *Fortune* magazine article by Geoff Colvin. The article provides three good examples of companies that continued investing despite the economic downturn. The chip-maker Qualcomm saw its profits plunge during the recession, yet it increased its research and development expenses every year. Intel invested considerable sums in new plant construction despite the reality that the industry was "on life support and credit markets were traumatized." Blue-chip company Coca-Cola never hesitated a moment building its brand throughout the downturn.[21]

The conclusion of the article is that smart companies continue to invest for long-term benefit, particularly in crucial areas like people and capabilities, even when the economy is volatile. Not succumbing to the daily pressures of short-term results takes real courage.

18. Cost Mind-Set

Strong leaders clearly understand that the organization must be fanatical about controlling costs. They also understand that cost control is cultural, not structural, and that this bias must be supported with the appropriate internal process mechanisms and embedded into the company's cultural DNA. Moreover, this culturally focused cost mind-set must transcend all economic environments.

19. Ability to Build an Enduring Enterprise

Visionary leaders focus on building an organization that will last. I believe this is best done by vigorously implementing the nine lifelines outlined in this book. As such, these leaders work hard to build these nine crucial lifelines during good times so that when they encounter dark days filled with uncertainty and volatility, they and their organizations will thrive and outperform unprepared enterprises.

Intuitive leaders know that this work is an insurance policy against the hard times that are sure to emerge in the future. These are some examples of such investments:

» training and development of the team so that they are well prepared for any crisis

» upgrading infrastructure (mainly technology) so that efficiency is built into an organization's standard processes

» research and development (innovation and science) investment made wisely and effectively to provide a competitive advantage that sustains the company

» developing an innovative business model that provides a competitive advantage

» building exceptional capabilities that provide a distinct competitive advantage

» building cash reserves for surviving a downturn and for taking advantage of the opportunities created as a result of economic downturns and global shocks

» paying down debt so that the company has maximum flexibility and liquidity

» rebalancing the portfolio to reduce market concentration, geographic concentration, and customer concentration risk

» building a flexible and variable cost structure that can be recalibrated based on economic activity

» other mission-critical initiatives that strengthen the company for the long-term

A leader who exemplified this mind-set was Steve Jobs. He obsessed over building as much cash as possible for a rainy day. He was also strongly against taking on any debt and using precious cash resources for share repurchases. Another exceptional leader who exemplified the mind-set of building cash reserves to take advantage of opportunities during severe economic downturns is Warren Buffett, the sage. In an October 7, 2013, *Wall Street Journal* article, Anupreeta Das highlighted this extraordinary skill, which is captured brilliantly in the title "Buffett's Crisis-Lending Haul Reaches $10 Billion." The article recounts how Buffett provided crucial cash to a handful of blue-chip companies at the height of the crisis in 2008 and how "five years later, the payoff on those deals is becoming clear: $10 billion and counting." The article goes on to state that "few investors, if any, capitalized on the crisis as expertly."[22]

Effective leaders skillfully balance a long-term perspective with short-term needs. This is no easy task, and it requires a leader with vision, courage, and fortitude. These leaders are capable of rallying the team to deliver short-term results when necessary, while planning and executing a long-term vision. These leaders do not buckle to short-term pressure but stay committed to the long-term sustainability and health of the organization.

Example: Sustainable Mind-Set

A leader who exemplified a long-term sustainability mind-set during his leadership tenure was Jack Welch, former CEO of General Electric.

In *Jack: Straight from the Gut*, cowritten with John Byrne, Welch recalls that when he was elected CEO, he implemented a transformation strategy that included a requirement that all businesses in the portfolio be ranked number one or two without exception. As a consequence of this strategy, General Electric divested itself of a number of businesses.

During this process, Welch established an important principle for the company. The principle was that any gains resulting from divestitures would be used to improve the company's competitiveness by reinvesting for the future. In other words, the gains would not provide a one-time earnings benefit but would be used as an offset to charges recorded to improve the remaining businesses. He followed this principle for decades, and it was instrumental in helping him achieve his goal of delivering consistent earnings growth.

---

20. Generative Thinking

Outstanding leaders are generative thinkers. That is, they take time to step back and examine the global landscape and look at economic, political, and end-market trends that could potentially impact the long-term health of the company—for example, the consideration of key emerging economies like China, India, Brazil, Russia, Turkey, Indonesia, Saudi Arabia, Mexico, and South Africa and the potential near- and long-term impact of these countries, particularly China, on the global economy. World population growth and the potential increased need for water, food, energy, and infrastructure is another target for generative thinking. Consideration of current geopolitical circumstances (where the position of the United States as undisputed global leader is being challenged) and the impact this circumstance might have on an enterprise is another example. Generative thinking needs to be an integral part of developing a company's envisioned future and a strategy for building lifelines.

21. Continuous Self-Improvement

Self-improvement is well exemplified by mountaineering. In their book *Extreme Alpinism: Climbing Light, Fast, and High*, authors Mark F. Twight and James Martin state:

> Great climbers remake themselves. They pare away impediments from life on the ground and cast a new character suited for the challenges ahead. Although born with an internal fire, they temper that fire with the recognition that only an unsentimental view of them will show where they need to improve and learn. Once they see the path to their goals, they adhere to it despite setbacks and difficulty.[23]

Precocious leaders passionately believe in continuous self-improvement and are disciplined in improving both their mental and physical capacity. As such, they closely follow national and international current events and trends while carefully monitoring the global political and business environment. These leaders are also passionate about maintaining a healthy lifestyle, and they fully embrace learning and self-renewal.

22. Equanimity

Inspiring leaders are always cool, calm, and collected, and they exhibit clear thinking and quiet confidence no matter the situation. Their composure and steady hand under severe conditions sends a calming and reassuring message to the entire enterprise. President Abraham Lincoln has a reputation for having exemplified this characteristic as he led the country through the Civil War.

23. Negotiating Skills

Accomplished leaders are smart negotiators who prepare before a key negotiation starts and skillfully navigate through the negotiation process once it begins. Successful leaders build credibility during the process and negotiate using sound judgment and compromise in a way that leads to a win-win conclusion.

The best negotiators enter the process with a deep understanding of the culture and background of the people involved in the negotiations. Substantial due diligence prior to commencing the negotiations may be required, especially when negotiating within the context of another culture. For example, the slow-moving technique of the Chinese may seem tedious and wearing when compared to the more direct Western approach. When negotiating within the Indian culture, it may be necessary to abandon all previous assumptions about negotiating to find a solution.

24. Gratefulness

Strong and successful leaders are grateful for what they've achieved and to the support team they lead. They understand that their achievements would not have happened without the steadfast commitment of others. The author Melody Beattie captured gratitude very well when she said, "Gratitude makes sense of our past, brings peace for today, and creates a vision for tomorrow."[24]

25. Giving Nature

Leaders need to live by positive example. Excellent leaders are involved in the community, and they commit to a lifetime of service. They are engaged with the community and provide leadership and resources to advance important local initiatives. They inspire young people to seek a career in business by demonstrating that financial success can be shared with the community and society as a whole. As such, these leaders are a true lifeline to help the younger generation in a community get on a right path in life.

As a leader, I am committed to assisting young people in starting their careers in business. I strongly backed Harsco's outreach activities throughout the world, supported internships for college students, and provided job opportunities for graduates. I also mentored and advised young people on business careers, and I spoke often at universities to inspire others to leadership positions.

26. Team-Building Talents

Skilled leaders have the ability to find and field a true A-team. Building a strong team takes instinct, judgment, perspective, and effective communication skills. Team building also requires consensus-building abilities that attract the best team members and an appreciation that a strong team can't be built without a well-developed leadership and talent-management system.

27. Accountability

The best leaders clearly understand that they are fully accountable, and they do not walk away from their responsibilities. Irrespective of the headwinds or particular circumstances, great leaders embrace and accept this responsibility. They manifest calmness and composure and are always magnanimous.

28. Perseverance

Remarkable leaders always persevere. They have an unwavering faith in their abilities and to those they lead in the organization. The great inventor Thomas Edison captured this characteristic well when he said, "Our greatest weakness lies in giving up. The most certain way to succeed is always to try just one more time."[25]

As explained earlier, during my fifty-month tenure as CEO, Harsco faced the most challenging business environment in its modern history. We were dramatically and adversely impacted by two extreme global economic shocks. These shocks weighed heavily on the performance of the company as revenues plunged 25 percent in one year and pricing pressures added an additional burden to the company's performance. Irrespective of the severe headwinds, the company persevered and executed its strategic plan. As a result, much was accomplished during this turbulent and difficult time, including a dramatic reduction to the cost structure, notable advancements in innovation, and the building of a substantial and successful business in China, India, and Latin America.

29. Survival Instincts

Like Alpine mountaineers, resourceful leaders possess strong survival skills. Leaders survive because they are proactive, disciplined, and keenly aware of threats. They plan properly for potentially catastrophic events by building an abundant number of lifelines. They move quickly to counteract threats and are vigilant, fully aware, and absolutely passionate about safety and self-rescue.

30. Learning, Teaching, and Coaching Ability

Finally, talented leaders understand that learning, teaching, and coaching are essential skills of a leader. Capable leaders learn from mistakes by performing an in-depth review of their performance. They do not assign blame for a mistake but take proactive action to ensure the mistake is not repeated. A leader's sole objective is to learn from both successful and unsuccessful experience. Former GE CEO Jack Welch had this to say about learning: "An organization's ability to learn, and translate that learning into action rapidly, is the ultimate competitive advantage."[26]

Exceptional leaders take every opportunity to teach team members.

Sage advice is the hallmark of a good leader. Leaders also coach the team with the objective of moving the organization forward.

Lifelines Inventory

In the book *Alpine Climbing: Techniques to Take You Higher,* authors Houston and Cosley make a compelling case for the importance of assessing your skills and knowledge, challenging the reader with questions:

> An honest and dispassionate self-critique is indispensable … How confident are you in your decisions and assessments? Is your confidence (or lack of it) justified by your level of skill and experience? What is your state of mind? What inner and outer factors might be affecting you at this moment, and might they threaten the quality of your decision-making ability?[27]

This chapter introduced you to the thirty precocious traits of extraordinary leaders. How many of these characteristics describe your leadership style or abilities? You should use this list to perform a leadership lifeline inventory. Here are some general guidelines for this assessment:

» Complete an assessment at least once per year and share your assessment with someone you trust to ensure that your self-assessment is completed objectively.

» Discuss your assessment with those who know you best and summarize the finding in a short "executive highlights" format to make the job easier.

» Develop a comprehensive and substantive action plan that addresses major shortcomings.

One recommended approach is using a professional coach to assist with the assessment. These professionals bring insight and an unbiased view to the assessment process. Another possibility is to ask for assistance from the human-resources group within your organization. Once this self-assessment and inner reflection are completed, you must follow through on the plan with discipline and focus.

Takeaways

Leaders today need to possess thirty specific characteristics to be successful. Some of these characteristics are innate while others are developed through the right character-building experiences, ongoing training, and focused commitment. The ultimate success of a leader will be determined by the depth and breadth of the leader's implementation of these characteristics. In this chapter, you learned about the thirty characteristics of exceptional leaders as restated below. Exceptional leaders

- » are paragons of integrity;

- » possess an ability to navigate a highly turbulent global environment while at the same time delivering strong performance, regardless of the economic climate;

- » practice equanimity and serve as strategist, coach, and team-builder;

- » demonstrate sound judgment consistently and always lead with passion, enthusiasm, and calmness;

- » inspire everyone in the organization, communicate effectively, and apologize effectively;

- » are humble but redoubtable;

- » commit to a lifetime of continuous self-improvement;

- » build extraordinary teams and demonstrate courage in all the decisions they make;

- » value facts, negotiate expertly across cultures, and build and implement leadership lifelines;

- » are strongly committed to the community, with a lifetime of service and giving; and

- » complete a lifelines inventory at least once a year to assess their strengths and weaknesses in order to continuously improve.

CHAPTER 2

Indispensable Experiences

The journey of a thousand miles begins with one step.
—Lao Tzu[28]

Perhaps the best way to explain the concept of indispensable experiences is to envision the path that newly appointed CEOs might have taken on their climb to the summit. What indispensable experiences might have been useful to position these new leaders for success? What processes, mechanisms, and strategies did they employ to reach the apex of their career? What lifelines were extended along the way that altered, for the better, their projected path?

Professional climbers are successful because they are deliberate about building the right climbing skills and choosing the right route to the summit. As a business leader, you must also choose the most strategically advantageous route, and you must possess the right set of strong skills that have been cumulatively developed through indispensable experiences. And, as the central metaphor in this book suggests, it is essential to consider where and when to attach your support lifeline to avoid unexpected calamities and "get down the mountain," as the second mountaineering rule admonishes. Remember, few leaders or individuals spend a lifetime at the top (with the exception of perhaps Warren Buffett), so everyone needs the right support lifelines going up and coming down from the career summit.

In their book *Alpine Climbing: Techniques to Take You Higher*, mountaineering authors Mark Houston and Kathy Cosley superbly capture the essence of climbing the summit, which offers a wonderful lens for viewing the business world. Here's a short excerpt that I think captures the challenges and the environment that leaders face as they endeavor to reach their personal summit (leadership goals):

> Mountains exert a mysterious power … They can fascinate, terrify, invite, or repel us … To climb a mountain is to enter a world where one's own insignificance and vulnerability are painfully obvious—a world that is indifferent to our desire to overcome its obstacles as it is to our survival … Our ability to explore this territory and come home safely depends on … understanding … the nature of the mountain environment … The fact is, we can survive in this environment if we approach it on its own terms, understanding the nature of the potential threats, recognizing them when we see them, and finding ways to avoid or reduce them. We must learn to perceive danger signs and stay out of the way of threatening events … We … minimize their impact by means of planning, action, and reaction based on awareness and understanding of the threat.[29]

Career-Building Experiences

Indispensable experiences shape and define every leader, but the most successful leaders (especially those who reach the top) deliberately acquire specific experiences through proactive actions they know will prepare and sustain them for their journey. These vital experiences are difficult to define, so I'll provide a few examples—augmented with some business insights—to demonstrate how the right personal experiences can shape a career.

So what are right experiences, and how do you construct a strategy to acquire them? From my perspective, applying the following set of criteria will help you determine the potential career benefit that might result from seeking out a particular experience. Look for experiences that have the following benefits:

» *Instructive and insightful.* Can you learn a lesson that will bring valuable wisdom and insight?

» *Developmental and character-building.* Will the experience bring professional and emotional growth?

» *Formative and impactful.* Can you clearly identify a resulting career-/life-shaping impact as a result of pursuing an experience?

» *Cultural and technical.* Will you gain an empathetic workforce lesson as well as build a specific, career-enhancing skill?

Note that both the scientist Albert Einstein and Roman emperor Julius Caesar were sold on the power of experience. Einstein offered that "the only source of knowledge is experience,"[30] while Julius Caesar was convinced that "experience is the teacher of all things."[31]

Support for Indispensable Experiences through Talent Management

Elite organizations usually have a disciplined and robust leadership-development and talent-management process for succession planning. In addition, these programs usually assign a suitable mentor to ensure a successful transition. Truly forward-thinking organizations go a step further to ensure that leaders also have all the necessary job experiences to support expected world-class job performance. These experiences include the following:

» *Stretch assignments.* Completion of one or more of these long-term assignments stretches a leader's abilities and allows him or her to lead through times of economic expansion and contraction. They include running a business unit, a segment of the company, or even the entire enterprise as president and/or chief operating officer.

» *Overseas experience.* In today's complex and difficult global business environment, it is difficult, if not impossible, to lead a multinational company without having a significant long-term overseas assignment.

» *Mentoring.* A mentor should be assigned as soon as an individual is identified as a high-potential candidate. One caveat regarding a mentor: my experience is that the informal mentoring relationships that occur naturally within an organization are much more successful than simply assigning someone a mentor through a bureaucratic process. If possible, a mentor from outside the organization should also be assigned.

» *Extensive training.* Ongoing internal and external training is an essential element in the development of future leaders. The training should include actual case studies, lessons learned, and extensive interaction with senior management.

Providing Essential Leadership Lifelines to New CEOs

New leaders need five key leadership lifelines once they take the reins of an enterprise as CEO or in another leadership position. The board of directors and the outgoing CEO have the obligation to take substantive and measurable action to ensure that the new leader is a success, which includes providing the following lifelines:

» *An experienced mentor.* The mentor can be the former leader, an executive coach, or possibly a senior board member. Often a retiring leader is not the right candidate to be a mentor because he or she may wish to provide the successor with a clear unobstructed path to perform the job. Executive coaches are one possible alternative; they are highly trained and skilled individuals who provide a fresh outside perspective that incorporates all past experiences from working with numerous executives. Another possibility for a mentor is a senior board member who previously served as a leader. As explained earlier, these relationships work better if they occur naturally and informally. In addition, it is wise for the newly appointed leader to visit with at least one sitting leader who is willing to share experiences. This confidential and unbiased view of what it's like to sit in the CEO chair is invaluable for the new leader—plus it offers a trusted lifeline.

» *Unwavering board of directors and executive team support.* The board of directors, executive team, and retiring leader must create the proper support environment to give the new leader the best opportunity for success. This means complete board transparency and sage advice based on their unique inside perspective. The transition support team must also avoid politics and never take any actions that might undermine the new leader's position.

» *Appropriate training.* A newly appointed CEO should be offered (and perhaps required to attend) training specifically tailored for the new leadership role—for example, Harvard University's strong program exclusively designed for new CEOs.

» *An outside relationship with a trusted confidant.* The leader should develop a relationship with an outside, independent partner who is a good and trusted generative thinker. As explained in chapter 3, "Proactive Actions," I developed an outside relationship with Jim Collins, whose advice was immensely helpful during my tenure as CEO of Harsco.

» *A position on the board of directors of another company.* This is a must for the development of the new leader. The experience provides numerous benefits, but the most important is an inside look at how other boards and enterprises operate and exposure to a diverse group of leaders and their perspectives.

Leaders with this solid foundation of broad experiences and strong support are more likely to succeed. Everyone involved in the succession-planning process must contribute to this effort, particularly if transitioning to a new CEO. However, you must remember that at the end of the day, the board of directors is ultimately responsible for the success of the CEO, so this group must take a leading role in the effort.

Case Studies of Indispensable Experiences

It is fine to offer pointers for grooming new leaders and to support gaining career-defining experiences, but I think the best way to explain these concepts is through case studies. What follows are two such examples. One case study is a review of the experiences of legendary leader Louis V. Gerstner Jr. of IBM, and the other is my own experience of achieving the top leadership position at Harsco. Both offer insight into the principle that it is difficult, if not impossible, to reach the summit without the right experiences.

Who Says Elephants Can't Dance?

Gerstner's penetrating book *Who Says Elephants Can't Dance?*[32] is a powerful account of how he reinvented and transformed IBM and established the foundation for sustainable growth. Gerstner's rescue and transformation of IBM makes him one of the top CEOs in history. A review of his work and life history quickly shows that without his particular set of right or indispensable experiences he would not have been chosen for leadership. So what were those indispensable experiences?

First, he had a stellar academic background. He attended Dartmouth and Harvard. His professional career equaled his academic background. He started at the management consulting firm McKinsey & Company and eventually became a senior partner. Gerstner said the most important experience "at McKinsey was the detailed process of understanding the underpinnings of a company. McKinsey was obsessive about deep analysis of a company's marketplace, its competitive position, and its strategic direction."[33]

Gerstner was recruited by his client, American Express, to join the company, and his experiences at American Express were also indispensable to his career:

> Early on I discovered, to my dismay, that the open exchange of ideas ... doesn't work so easily in a large, hierarchical-based organization. ... Thus began a lifelong process of trying to build organizations that allow for

hierarchy but at the same time bring people together for problem solving, regardless of where they are positioned within the organization. It was also at American Express that I developed a sense of the strategic value of information technology.[34]

Gerstner left American Express to take on the challenges of RJR Nabisco, which had been formed through the merger of Nabisco and R. J. Reynolds Tobacco Company. Just as at McKinsey and American Express, Gerstner learned many valuable lessons at RJR Nabisco. Gerstner says he "came away from this experience with a profound appreciation of the importance of cash in corporate performance—free cash flow as the single most important measure of corporate soundness and performance ... I came away with a greater sense of the relationship between management and owners."[35]

As you can see, Gerstner's experiences were all truly indispensable and prepared him well for his ultimate challenge at IBM.

My Essential Career Lifelines

During my career, I had the privilege and honor to work with many talented individuals. All of them made a notable contribution to the success of the company. There were three talented and exceptional senior executives who took a particular interest in my career, and they were responsible for providing me with essential opportunities that ultimately resulted in indispensable experiences.

The first mentor was the person who hired me. He gave me an opportunity to develop and grow, and he was responsible for my early promotions. A second mentor was responsible for my promotion to senior positions, including CEO. Without these two individuals, I would not have had the required indispensable experiences that allowed me to reach the ultimate summit of a business career. The third person was an operating executive who was very supportive, particularly when I was CFO and president. These three individuals provided crucial lifelines as I successfully climbed each summit during my career.

The final important mentor to me was a board member who retired prior to my taking over as CEO. He possessed all the positive attributes of a successful leader. I was fortunate to develop a strong bond before he retired, and this bond became an important lifeline that eventually led to the board member becoming my mentor—a role of providing sage advice and friendship that continues even today.

My Journey, from the Beginning

My first indispensable experience was when I landed my first job at age seven chasing tennis balls at a resort hotel in Rapallo, Italy. The money wasn't bad for a seven-year-old, although I had to turn all earnings over to my mother as my contribution to keeping the family fed and the bills paid. I really enjoyed my job, and even at this early age I learned the power of providing a high-quality service and how doing so is directly connected to improved earnings.

After my family moved to the United States in 1961, I had a newspaper route during the 1960s that I kept until I graduated from high school. The job required the formation of strong, disciplined habits and was in many ways the foundation for my business career. Not only did my newspaper route offer a marvelous lesson in running a small business, it was truly an entrepreneurial enterprise. You had total control of your business, including cash management and customer service, both of which determined your success or failure. You also had to be a bit Machiavellian about customer service. You knew that good customer service today would result in a bigger carrier bonus during Christmas. For example, I would ask each customer what time and where they wanted their paper delivered (on the doorstep, front porch, etc.) and even how they wanted it folded. Paying attention to all these details paid direct Christmas-bonus dividends from my happy customers.

I also had a myriad of other jobs growing up, including stocking and managing shelves at a local grocery store, making pizza at a movie drive-in, working at a paper factory, and learning about the restaurant business on a street lunch truck. The grocery-store job taught me how to manage inventory, market products, and maintain accurate records. My paper-manufacturing-plant job was physically difficult, and it gave me an appreciation of how hard some people work in factories for minimal compensation. It also motivated me to seek a different career path. The pizza-making job was the easiest because I got to watch movies while doing something that I love, cooking.

However, of all these jobs, my relative's lunch truck was the most memorable and ultimately the most significant. The day started at six thirty in the morning, when we'd load the truck with enough provisions for numerous scheduled stops throughout my hometown of Harrisburg, Pennsylvania. The last stop at Harrisburg Steel in downtown Harrisburg was at one in the afternoon and always had the largest number of customers. What is perhaps most interesting—and a little eerie—is that my future employer, Harsco, began its business in 1853 in this same facility.

Living the American Dream

After graduating from Pennsylvania State University (Harrisburg), I worked as an auditor for three years, and during that time at the auditor general's office, I earned a certified public accountant (CPA) and later a certified information systems auditor (CISA) certificate. I was hired by Harsco as an internal auditor in the summer of 1980 and rose over the next thirty-two years from an entry-level auditor position to ultimately president, CEO, and chairman. That's the top-line story, but a little more detail is required to serve the purpose of this book.

My Career Lifelines

Certain lifelines were extended to me during my early years that were essential to obtaining the right experiences. However, I also created my own lifelines through hard work, discipline, and commitment to always getting the job done right. And as noted in the recounting of the history of my work life, all these essential experiences converge to create the leaders we become later in our careers.

Hard work is usually easy to observe and is often noticed by people you may not even know. I was lucky to work on many key projects throughout my career, such as large acquisitions, major divestitures, transformational joint ventures, and other strategic initiatives. In all these assignments, I did what had to be done, which meant extensive travel, working extremely long hours, and sometimes going long periods without a day off. Colleagues told me that I consistently delivered good results and worked well in a team environment.

One particular person did take notice, and he eventually became the Harsco CEO and, of course, an important lifeline who I faithfully served in various capacities for more than twenty years. This key lifeline ultimately recommended me for the CEO position, and I expressed my gratitude and appreciation through hard work, strong results, and loyalty. Together we transformed the company and achieved many years of record results while creating substantial shareholder value along the way.

First Senior-Management Exposure

In the mideighties, I was appointed to be director of internal audit. It was my first meaningful exposure to senior management at a time when Harsco was going through a major transformation brought about by acquisition and divestiture activities. Since we handled the majority of the due-diligence work on acquisitions and oversaw major aspects of the divestitures, the audit group was a focal point in the deals. Our group's performance during this time got the attention of senior management, and in particular the senior team noticed the unveiling of Harsco's integrated audit approach.

At the time, this was an innovative way to perform internal audits that brought together all financial and operational audits under one integrated program. The system also integrated our internal audit work with that of external audits performed by our independent accountants. This system achieved significant efficiencies that not only lowered audit fees but also allowed us to perform more work. The paper I wrote for *Management Accounting* magazine in January 1988[36] brought positive attention and ultimately was a factor in my promotion to corporate controller.

One of the first recommendations I made in the position of corporate controller in the early nineties was a reinvention of our closing process through innovation. Our closing process was very long and manually focused. I presented the idea to our CFO and CEO, and they tasked me with leading the project. My first step on the road to this process reinvention was to contact Motorola and AMP (now TE Connectivity), companies considered at the time to be global leaders in process improvement and innovative closing processes. Both companies had fine-tuned their financial closing process so that it took just a few days. By comparison, Harsco at the time needed about fifteen days to close its books.

After gaining invaluable insights by attending a Motorola Six-Sigma program, I visited AMP to study the software program that allowed the company to close its global books so quickly. Ultimately, I used what I learned to introduce a continuous process improvement that included modern software and technology-driven automating processes that shortened the closing process from fifteen days to five days. We later reduced the days to four, and that process is still in place twenty years later.

In 1994, I wrote and developed an internally published booklet titled *Harsco Internal Control Framework* that established minimum global standards of internal control across the enterprise. The CEOs and CFOs were required to certify the validity of their financial statements and associated internal controls as part of the process. The document was later used by the global finance team as the foundation for implementing the requirements of Sarbanes-Oxley law (2002) because the law had similar but more expansive requirements.

In 1998, I was appointed CFO of Harsco and served in that position for ten years. My tenure there was characterized by superior results and team support. Specifically, our success was characterized by the following:

1. Strong, record results

2. Loyalty to the CEO and my ability to communicate effectively in a frank and candid way on matters of strategy and personnel

3. Focus on building a strong balance sheet underpinned by strong cash flows

4. Focus on improving the quality of the global finance group (that group became a consistent top-tier performer in the company)

5. An ability to consistently execute on strategic initiatives and deliver on my commitments

As a consequence, I was rewarded in 2002 with an appointment to the board of directors and in 2006 to the position of president of the company.

My promotion to president (and CFO) in January 2006 was the ultimate test. The most notable achievement of the team during my two years as president was the record increase in sales, income, cash flow, and shareholder value. This performance paved the way for my appointment to CEO and the reaching of my personal summit.

During my career, I was fortunate to be involved, in various capacities, in many major strategic transformations that provided deep perspective and the necessary skills to conduct and oversee future transformations. All my predecessors had done an excellent job of transforming and reinventing the company since its founding, and this ability to reinvent itself remained an enduring characteristic of Harsco. Every transformation journey was a success, resulting in improved performance and increased shareholder value. Valuable lessons were learned from my predecessors and from experiencing these transformations firsthand.

Key Indispensable Experiences

I traveled extensively throughout the world during my career, and I gained invaluable perspective on different cultures and various new and innovative business models. I also met some exceptional people in my journey. Here are five experiences that particularly stand out, as well as several memorable experiences in my post-Harsco professional period. These experiences demonstrate the positive effect of creating meaningful and substantive experiences.

Harsco's Fiftieth Anniversary Celebration

In 2006, to celebrate Harsco's fifty years on the New York Stock Exchange, I was allowed to participate as president of the company in ringing the closing bell. While this is indeed a memorable event, what really made the event special was the fact that my friends and relatives in my birthplace of Mammola, Italy, watched the event on television. I realized that I had become an inspirational figure for perhaps another poor kid with dreams of something better.

Journey to Italy as CEO and Chairman

This impression was confirmed every time I traveled to Italy on business as the CEO and chairman of the company. I was amazed at the respect and adulation I received. People were so proud that a *contadino* (peasant) from Calabria could achieve this position.

World Connections That Make a Difference

The Chinese people admire those who run large enterprises. I experienced this everywhere I went in China. I developed a strong bond with some Chinese business leaders, including the chairman of the largest stainless-steel company in the world, which is based in Shanxi province. We ultimately collaborated on developing a technology that not only recycled essentially 100 percent of a certain waste stream but also used the by-product in an innovative way. I was very proud of this substantial business achievement but also proud because it created a new business model of working with the Chinese centered on the environment.

Another memorable aspect of this important global connection was the groundbreaking ceremony I attended in China along with many Chinese and American dignitaries. The speech that I gave at the ceremony was one of my most important. Here is what I said:

> It is an honor and a privilege to be here today. A good friend of Harsco once told me that not all time in life is equal. There are moments in life that are significantly more important than others, and thus they need to be cherished. Clearly, this event is one of those unequal moments. We are here today to symbolically plant the seed from which will grow a strong and enduring partnership. Our two great companies are joining forces to build and develop a business that not only protects the environment but also advances technology and global best practices. We at Harsco are honored, and we are proud, to say the TISCO is our partner.

Opportunity to Share Experiences

An invitation to speak at the Tuck School of Business at Dartmouth College from Professor Richard A. D'Aveni was a particularly rewarding event. Sharing my experience with graduate students from one of the top business schools in the world was a stupendous honor, especially since I don't have an MBA. I had a private meeting with the dean of the business school, a private lunch with about six students who asked uncensored questions. I spoke to two different classes about business transformations and strategy. Importantly, Professor D'Aveni later spoke to the global leadership team at our annual offsite meeting and our connection led to me writing a short piece for his book *Strategic Capitalism: The New Economic Strategy for Winning the Capitalist Cold War.*

Connections to Leading Business Experts

Over a fifty-month period, I was fortunate to form a connection with business-management guru Jim Collins and spend time with him at his lab in Boulder, Colorado. Jim Collins is highly intelligent, gifted writer, but he is much, much more. He is humble, inspirational, insightful, visionary, and simply a wonderful person. On my first visit with him, he asked me to review the draft manuscript to his new book at the time, *How the Mighty Fall,* and later added my name to his acknowledgments in his book *Great by Choice.*

New Summits to Climb

What I discovered after separating from the company is that there is indeed life after leading a 20,000-person organization. The world does not come to an end; this is a lesson learned that leaders need to clearly understand and appreciate. There are new frontiers ready to be explored and new personal summits to climb. As a result of my separation, I joined several companies as a member of their board of directors. I engaged and established a relationship with a private equity group, and I wrote two books and started my own business. As a consequence, new horizons were explored and new perspectives were gained. All of these new indispensable experiences have enriched my life and made me a better leader.

Without these indispensable experiences, my journey to the summit would have followed a completely different path, and perhaps I wouldn't have reached the top at all.

Takeaways

The takeaway message is that we need to have audacious dreams when we are young because anything is possible. Dream big—no vision is too large! The opportunities for indispensable experiences are immense; it is up to us to capitalize on them. Here are some other key lessons from this chapter:

» The right experiences are essential for a successful climb to the summit. We are defined by the accumulation of these crucial experiences. The right experiences are instructive and insightful; developmental and character-building; formative and impactful; and cultural and technical. These indispensable experiences will prepare you for your personal ascent to your career summit.

» Organizations need to ensure that future star leaders are identified and provided with the right essential experiences through a vigorous, experience-focused leadership-development and talent-management system.

» Enterprises must ensure that newly appointed leaders or CEOs are well-trained and equipped to deal with the strenuous requirements of the position and are provided with an appropriate number of indispensable experiences to increase the probability of success.

CHAPTER 3

Proactive Actions

Do you want to know who you are? Don't ask. Act!
Action will delineate and define you.
—Thomas Jefferson[37]

As demonstrated throughout this book, the climb to the summit is arduous, and only a proactive mind-set—along with just the right dash of luck and talent—will increase your probability of success. Leaders must adequately prepare every day for their climb to the summit. This can be accomplished by following the recipe for success outlined in this chapter. It is important for leaders to remember that the recipe works throughout an entire career, as each summit is climbed.

In this chapter, we will examine proactive actions through the lens of a newly appointed CEO or other high-level leadership position with similar responsibilities. However, many of the salient points covered here have broad applicability to leaders of all types of organizations, including the leader of a sales team, a business unit, or an entire division. What is important is that the recipe for success through proactive actions is followed.

CEO Leadership Tenure Is Ephemeral

As discussed in the preface, the average tenure of a Fortune 500 CEO today is fifty-four months due mainly to a hypercompetitive global economy and changing attitudes (both inside and outside the organization) about assigning blame for failure.

An article published by the *Conference Board Review*[38] points out that CEOs are increasingly being blamed for all company failures, irrespective of the turbulence in the global economy or local end-market conditions. This public intolerance is reflected in impatience at the shareholder and board level, and this serves only to increase the pressures of managing a global business successfully.

CEOs today face a conundrum as a result of these external and internal pressures. Clearly, these leaders understand that they are responsible for both the long-term and short-term health of their company, but it is a difficult balance to strike. This point is made in a memorandum by Martin Lipton and several others who are experts on corporate governance. Here is what they said in late 2012:

> The years since the onset of the financial crisis have served to further increase the demands on and scrutiny of public company boards of directors. The assault on the director-centric model of corporate governance continues in the shareholder activist and political arenas, and the challenges of planning for and investing in the long-term health of the corporation have become more daunting. As the power and organization of both governance and hedge-fund activists have increased, the pressure to produce short-term results has only grown stronger, regardless of whether the steps necessary to produce those results may be harmful to the corporation in the long run.[39]

That same year, *Fortune* magazine published a survey titled "Tenure at the Top: How Long Is Too Long (or Too Short) for a CEO to Lead a Company?"[40] The findings are based on a survey from one hundred public companies. Although the study is focused on large companies, I believe that the findings can likely be extrapolated to the top one thousand companies.

There are several salient points from the survey. First, "Brief CEO tenures (five or fewer years) tend to be an equal mix of positive and negative returns. That changes at about the seven-year mark, as companies with positive returns outweigh those with negative returns."

This is an interesting comment, and it is consistent with my experience that it typically takes about seven years for a CEO to completely transition into the position and to implement his strategic vision for the company. The survey goes on to say that "the ideal CEO tenure tends to be between 10 and 15 years." Again, a finding that is consistent with my experience, as my predecessor enjoyed a fourteen-year tenure. The obvious question here is, given current conditions, will CEOs be given the opportunity to fully grow into the position and its demands? I would argue that in many cases the answer is no! Unless there is another long period of sustained economic prosperity throughout the world, CEOs' tenure will continue to be precarious.

Finally, there is one other interesting finding from the *Fortune* magazine survey that supports my hypothesis that it is better to promote homegrown talent, particularly for the CEO position. Although this topic is discussed in substantial detail later in chapter 5, "Learning Entity," and chapter 7, "People Excellence," one point is salient to this discussion. According to the survey, "Homegrown talent fares better at the top than a hired gun might. CEOs with experience in the industry or company they lead are less likely to be forced out than outsiders and are more likely to post healthy returns to shareholders."

With this information as background, what follows is my recipe for the proactive actions that newly appointed leaders must take to survive the numerous and inevitable external and internal crisis situations they will surely face during their tenure.

A Recipe for Success through Proactive Actions

As stated earlier, it is important for leaders to remember that the recipe for success through proactive actions works throughout an entire career.

Here are the key ingredients of this successful recipe. A leader must do the following:

- » possess a proactive mind-set
- » develop a road map of proactive actions, with key inputs including inventory and assessment of lifelines as well as individual precocious characteristics
- » build an appropriate number of lifelines by networking and reaching out to key individuals and organizations
- » cultivate indispensable experiences through proactive action
- » focus on learning and continuous self-improvement
- » protect his or her reputation
- » take certain basic proactive actions when assuming a new leadership position (signing an appropriate agreement, appointing a chief human-resources officer, and gaining an improved perspective through learning)
- » implement the ten critical proactive actions once appointed as a leader
- » implement certain specific proactive actions after one year in a leadership position (appointment to an outside board position, 360 review, and feedback from key board members)

Overview and the Need for Proactive Actions

First, the old saying that "it's lonely at the top" is true, particularly if you are a new CEO. Once you've risen to the top of the organization, you must take certain crucial actions immediately as a proactive leader.

First, complete an inventory and assessment of all lifelines as discussed in the book. Once this is completed, develop a road map that identifies all required proactive actions. Fully utilize all of your precocious personal characteristics to develop the plan. These proactive actions will increase the probability of your success and serve to protect your reputation. Specifically, you'll need to build and begin implementing an abundant number of lifelines that address the particular needs of a new leader. Remember that these actions are acutely important if few lifelines are made available to you as a newly appointed leader. You will need to create and build your own by following all the steps outlined in this chapter.

One of your first proactive actions should be to reach out and network with key individuals and organizations to ensure that important lifelines are built early in your tenure. For example, you should contact other sitting CEOs and top leaders of elite organizations to seek valuable insight and advice and to open the door for possible benchmarking and other learning opportunities. Another effective action is to contact recently retired leaders. Not only are these leaders a wonderful source of information, they are also potential mentors. Again, this potential lifeline can create opportunities for learning and indispensable experiences.

Other possible proactive actions you'll need to explore include seeking out board positions, joining a prestigious national institution, establishing a relationship with a university, and reading as much material as possible on the subject of leadership (*Harvard Business Review* has excellent material). The possibilities for learning are endless, but the most important aspect is to be proactive and deliberate in the actions you take.

Personal Lifelines Developed through Proactive Actions—My Journey

Growing up, I often manifested a curious mind, and I was consistently proactive, as evidenced by the numerous jobs I mentioned in chapter 2, "Indispensable Experiences." In all these experiences, valuable lessons were learned and personal lifelines were built through each proactive action. My curiosity expanded in my teenage years. I learned to play the guitar and read music and studied Eastern civilization and its philosophy.

I also took a particularly deep interest in Isshin-Ryu Karate, which is an oriental martial-arts discipline that was developed over many centuries in Asia. What drew me to karate was not the obvious self-defense aspect but the values of refinement of character and spiritual fitness. The belief is that the individual should strive for a strong body and peace of mind. The true meaning of Isshin-Ryu Karate is found in its symbol of a half-female, half-dragon figure adorned with stars on a gray background. The female represents a quiet, peaceful character with strength to repel evil. The stars and gray background represent a calm and quiet night and underscore the discipline's use as a defense.

The dragon under Asian legend represents God rising from sea to sky. The Isshin-Ryu Karate symbol in essence represents God, mind, calm, and quiet strength. The most important teaching, however, is discipline and the need to avoid conflict unless there is a direct threat from which there is no escape or avoidance.

One of my key proactively developed personal lifelines was an ability to be consistently disciplined in my career approach. This was accomplished through continuous self-improvement initiatives, such as my study of Eastern civilization. My approach to continuous self-improvement was just part of a lifetime of learning and self-renewal. During my entire career, I improved my skills and knowledge base by taking additional college courses, attending targeted seminars, and studying and focusing on best practices.

Joining meaningful national organizations that provide opportunities for personal growth has been another effective means of self-improvement. I joined a prestigious national organization called Manufacturers Alliance for Productivity and Innovation (MAPI), and this action allowed me to visit other companies that opened some important doors in my career by providing me access to talented peers around the country. Through this access, I was exposed to and learned current best practices that improved and added to not only my overall skill set but also that of my employer.

Through proactive actions, I connected with two universities, Susquehanna University and Pennsylvania State University (Harrisburg). My interaction with academia gave me a different perspective on the world and helped in my overall development as a leader. Diverse experiences and perspectives are crucial for a leader, and I benefited from my many years of association with these two exceptional universities.

The final part of my self-renewal discipline was that every weekend, usually early in the morning, I devoted about four hours to reading business and technical literature (magazines, newspapers, and books). I had two objectives with this weekly ritual. First, it expanded my overall business leadership and technical knowledge. Second, I learned about important economic and geopolitical trends that could impact me and my company. It is incredible how you can detect important trends by this technique, but it requires discipline and generative thinking. I did this every weekend during my entire career, and I continue to do so today.

I also made it a point throughout my career to network and reach out to all types of leaders and professionals. It is always amazing how responsive people are when you ask them for assistance. Here is an example.

When I was appointed CEO, I proactively reached out to the author and management guru Jim Collins for assistance with building our OneHarsco culture, which is covered in chapter 8, "Distinctive Culture." This proactive action resulted in an invitation from Jim Collins to meet with nine other business leaders for about two days to engage in a robust dialogue session. During those two days, we explored many cogent topics, such as CEO succession planning, leadership, and dealing with adversity. As a newly appointed CEO, I was fortunate to have this self-created lifeline as my orientation program, which ultimately became an indispensable experience.

The next section digs a little deeper into crucial proactive actions and recipe ingredients for success, from the basic actions of a newly appointed leader to the ten critical actions of a new leader to a close look at the specific actions leaders must take after one year on the job.

The Basics: Actions Newly Appointed CEOs Need to Take

Before anything else, a newly appointed leader must get a written agreement with the board. It is always a good idea to have a clear exit strategy, since this is the time, before you accept the position, when you have maximum leverage to negotiate as many favorable terms as possible. This is where your precocious skills are important. Make sure that you engage an experienced and highly qualified lawyer to assist with the terms and conditions of the agreement, and think through the things that are most important to you. Beyond all the standard financial matters like salary, annual incentive, long-term incentive, and other compensation items, make sure that you cover relocation costs and living costs, and negotiate a sign-up bonus—likely some form of equity because of the nature of the position. If the job is for a senior officer position or president of a large business segment, try to also negotiate some form of guaranteed cash bonus.

In the euphoria of signing up to lead a company, you are liable to overlook one important factor: What happens if there is a separation (unplanned exit)? Leaders must think this through very carefully and make sure that they control as much of their separation as possible. You should think about both the process and the most substantive issues you might face, including some contractual way of protecting your reputation.

As part of the agreement, as noted earlier, make sure that the board sponsors your attendance at a highly regarded business-school course or workshop designed exclusively for new CEOs. Insist on this development program, because it is an absolute must. Finally, make sure you are in alignment with the board on the role of the ex-CEO and the specific transition length and overall plan.

Now with the agreement in place and your new CEO orientation scheduled or already completed, your next action is to make sure you have the right chief human-resources officer (CHRO) in place. In today's environment, this is probably the most important position for a CEO to fill. A strong CHRO is imperative for the success of the company and the CEO. This individual will not only help you shape your leadership team but also offer valuable insight like a *consigliere* or trusted advisor. Do not compromise on this, because your CHRO may be the only person in the company, other than your mentor, who you can talk openly with about the organization's top executives.

While you are completing all these important fundamental tasks, it is imperative that you begin your discipline of reading and studying. I recommend starting with Jim Collins's four exceptional books, *Built to Last, Good to Great, How the Mighty Fall*, and *Great by Choice*. These books will provide an excellent perspective on what you will face as a leader, and they will stimulate thinking and reflection.

In addition, read *Understanding Michael Porter* by Joan Magretta. She does a masterful job of summarizing Porter's exhaustive and amazing work that spanned more than three decades. As the book states, it is the essential guide to competition and strategy. All of Porter's work should be read because his work is meaningful and insightful. It is even more relevant today because of global tumult and fierce competition.

There are books from four great CEOs that should be read by all leaders. All four CEOs should be closely studied because there is so much that can be learned, starting with Louis V. Gerstner Jr., who I mentioned back in chapter 2, "Indispensable Experiences." The importance of corporate culture, which is often not well understood, is the main takeaway message from Gerstner's book, *Who Says Elephants Can't Dance?* I particularly liked Jack Welch's original book on his experiences as CEO of General Electric, *Jack: Straight from the Gut*, but I'd recommend reading all his other books as well. Procter & Gamble's CEO A. G. Lafley's book *Playing to Win: How Strategy Really Works* is another fundamental book that should be read. And finally, Fred Hassan's book, *Reinvent: A Leader's Playbook for Serial Success*, provides insight and perspective on turnarounds and transformations. Here are some other indispensable reads to put on your list:

» *Beating the Commodity Trap* by Richard A. D'Aveni. This book provides an interesting framework to spot the signs of creeping commoditization.

» *Strategic Capitalism: The New Economic Strategy for Winning the Capitalist Cold War* by Richard A. D'Aveni. This engrossing read will give you a broad overview of the potential impact of global economic and political upheaval and change.

» *Every Nation for Itself* by Ian Bremmer. This book by a world-renowned geopolitical analyst is a valuable and recommended companion to Richard A. D'Aveni's books.

» *Steve Jobs* by Walter Isaacson. This is a book that every newly appointed leader should read. It is an inspirational account of one of the greatest CEOs in history. There are numerous illuminating examples of the power of going with your instinct. The book also includes many lessons learned.

The Ten Critical Proactive Actions
for Newly Appointed CEOs

1. Review All Projects and Strategies

As a new leader, it is vital to complete a comprehensive review of all ongoing projects as well as the strategies the company has been following. Have each directly responsible team and team leader participate with you in an in-depth review of what they are doing. As we discovered during our "Good to Great" lab sessions, it is more powerful and effective to conduct a robust face-to-face dialogue session than sitting and listening to a formal presentation.

Vigorous dialogue sessions usually produce good results because they require knowledge, wisdom, and the ability to think. Although there is a time and place for formal presentations, this is not one of them. With this format, you achieve three constructive things. First, you learn more about those presenting and their ability to articulate their knowledge of the business without any mental crutches, such as a PowerPoint presentation. Second, this format makes you a better listener because you need to grasp and process quickly what is being said, and it tests your ability to take good notes. And third, this approach creates a better environment for team-building and working together.

2. Focus on the Customer and Meet with Investors

The customers and shareholders of the company are clearly a primary focus area for a new leader. Develop a high-priority, well-planned strategy early to visit all key customers throughout the world. The focus of each visit is primarily on listening and learning, and importantly, the visits are an opportunity for the leader to view his company through the lens of the customer. These visits are also an opportunity to build relationships that may have been previously ignored or taken for granted. Since taking action is a priority, any identified customer issues or follow-up promises made during the visit need to be addressed expeditiously.

If the CEO leads a public company, meeting with key shareholders must also be a high-priority proactive action. Investors must be reassured, through a scripted message, about the direction and strategy of the company.

3. Develop a Strategic Road Map, Envisioned Future, and Key Performance Metric

Getting the board of directors to fully engage in the development of the strategic road map and envisioned future of the company is another highly important matter to address right from the beginning. Total alignment and understanding now will prevent misunderstandings later in your tenure as CEO.

Your first step in this endeavor is to write a detailed memorandum to the board identifying the major challenges and opportunities facing the company, and most importantly how they will be addressed. This document can be used for the dialogue sessions with the board in developing the antidote and countermeasures needed to address all the challenges and strategies and seize the opportunities. The strategic dialogue must include a discussion of the short-term situation (five years) and a long-term envisioned future (twenty years).

That's why it is critical for a newly appointed CEO to have total clarity and full engagement from the board so that there is no ambiguity. A new leader cannot take the risk of a misunderstanding. As Booz & Company pointed out in a paper on lessons for new CEOs, "Board members need to take part in the strategic conversation as it develops; otherwise, they may overly focus on risk mitigation, a hallmark of inexperienced and uninformed boards."[41]

The most important part of this process is to get in advance and in writing what metric or metrics the board will use to measure the performance of the new leader. It is essential to reduce to a minimum the subjective measurement criteria of the overall performance of the executive.

As a regular discipline, a CEO should send a monthly report to the board on the status of the strategic road map and the envisioned future. Once a year, the leader should provide the board with a detailed progress report card. Also, at the annual strategy meeting with the board, all changes—particularly to the road map—should be documented to keep all members aligned. Maintain copious notes and modify the road map as necessary.

Once there is alignment with the board on the strategic road map and envisioned future, embark on a vigorous communication strategy. The communication from the CEO needs to be passionate, clear, and specific. Use a collection of modern media to get the message across. Do not rely on direct reports to get your personal message out. Don't run the risk of your message being filtered or, worse, being improperly communicated. Visit employees in the field so that they understand firsthand where the company is going to ensure they are aligned with your vision. Do not delegate this.

You will need a communication plan for the outside world as well, particularly for shareholders and the investment community. Establish credibility with all the various constituencies and be disciplined in the delivery of your commitment when delivering both good and bad news. Seriously consider retaining an outside public-relations firm to assist with the communication strategy.

4. Establish the CEO Relationship and Understand the Role of the Board

To say that the CEO relationship with the board is complex is an understatement. It takes skill and experience to navigate through this relationship, and newly appointed CEOs need a lifeline to help them manage this potentially difficult interaction. If available, one of the best sources of help is the former CEO. Newly appointed CEOs without this lifeline are more likely to make mistakes with the board.

To avoid missteps, leaders need to clearly understand the board's role and purpose. In general, boards have three high-level and critical tasks: overseeing the CEO and related succession planning, determining the strategy of the enterprise, and managing risk. Obviously, boards have other duties like executive compensation; compliance and corporate governance; navigating through a crisis or turbulence; and monitoring performance. The three duties mentioned above, however, are clearly the most important.

For CEOs, managing a relationship with the board is one of their most important tasks. The connections to the board a CEO must manage well include the following:

» *Board composition.* Most boards today are composed of accomplished and experienced individuals. The days of packing the board with local friends of the CEO are long gone. Although every board is different, one thing is certain, and that is that every board will have strong personalities. If the board has too many of these personality types, the CEO's tenure will be difficult, so it's essential to clearly understand these personalities and develop an appropriate strategy for the situation.

» *Matters arising.* A CEO should not assume anything. You need to ensure that appropriate mechanisms are in place to provide measured feedback to the board on all matters raised. A good mechanism for this is having minutes taken of each meeting with a section dedicated entirely to matters to be addressed. All these items must be followed up on and reported back to all the board members in writing. This is also a smart and pragmatic way for the leader to avoid any potential misunderstanding. Ignoring or not fully considering any matters arising is not a good idea, since these instances will be seen as snubs and might be cited as an example of CEO nonperformance later on.

» *Management responsibility.* Experienced and seasoned board members understand their role and that of management. They clearly know that the responsibility for managing the business resides with the CEO and the management team; they know that the board is responsible for overseeing their stewardship of the company. However, there are instances where certain board members cross that line and attempt to get involved in the management of the business. Regardless, if this occurs unintentionally or intentionally, CEOs need to guard against this type of behavior because it may undermine their authority.

Building critical lifelines, particularly with key directors, can be a powerful antidote to this type of behavior.

CEOs should formulate a separate strategy to deal with key board members, such as the lead director and the chairs of committees like audit, compensation, and governance/nominating. Again, it is important for the CEO to understand the personalities. Research the personalities and consider whether some might be possible lifelines. Even letters and other public documents written by a retired CEO can help you gain insight into a potential board member's thinking and management style.

In dealing with the board of directors, the CEO needs to be transparent and present a consistent and controlled message and also ensure total closure on all matters. Remember that the accountability and responsibility for the company is fully and squarely on the shoulders of the CEO, so it is vital for the leader to create as many lifelines as possible with the board. Here are some key lifelines to create:

» Minimize the number of changes to the board structure over a short period of time, particularly if you are facing a period of uncertainty and economic tumult. Don't underestimate the importance of this; proposed changes need to be thoroughly evaluated and considered.

» Develop a strong and transparent relationship with each committee chairperson. Gain their trust and loyalty. Communicate frequently. It is crucial that face-to-face meetings are scheduled on a regular basis. Make sure you market yourself. Do not assume that they will connect the dots and see things as you see them.

» There must be total clarity and alignment on strategy, risk, and succession planning with the board leaders. Again, this takes a considerable amount of effort from the CEO. Potent dialogue and transparency are key.

» The board must have an in-depth understanding of each business in the portfolio, including end-market dynamics and the competitive landscape. Do not underestimate the effort required to ensure that all board members, and particularly the leadership group, have a total grasp of the business. They need to have knowledge of the competitive landscape; end-markets; products and services; pricing dynamics; and strategies of each business. An effective mechanism is to have board members attend a multiday offsite management meeting so they can get an in-depth understanding of the business and its leadership. Site visits to business units should also be part of the training playbook.

» Create a comprehensive and vigorous communication plan for dealing with the board that is well thought out. It should include monthly written reports, periodic e-mail updates, and periodic telephone calls, particularly with each committee chairperson, and it should include a detailed feedback mechanism after each board meeting.

5. Pursue Change with Patience, Wisdom, and a High Level of Skepticism

As a new CEO, you need to be patient, particularly about change, although the passion and need for change will be difficult to control. Too much change can have negative consequences for you and the organization. Pick three absolute musts and focus on them. Communicate effectively. This is where precocious skills will help. It takes sound judgment and considerable wisdom to focus in on the three most important projects for the organization. The ability to instinctively choose the right path when there are so many roads is truly a gift.

Also, you need a high level of skepticism as a CEO. There is an old southern Italian proverb that goes like this: "Only believe half of what you see, and don't believe anything you hear." Do not take anything for granted. Do not assume anything; live by undisputed and unassailable facts, and back everything up with data. Conduct vigorous dialogue sessions. Go and see things for yourself, validate assumptions, and always rely on your instincts. As President Ronald Reagan once said about the Soviet Union, "Trust, but verify."[42] It is imperative that you develop and maintain the same type of mind-set.

6. *Employ Actions and Antidotes to Deal with CEO Surprises*

Harvard Business Review published a powerful paper titled "Seven Surprises for New CEOs."[43] It's a must-read for all new CEOs and for anyone else in a leadership position. Some of the findings you would expect, but others are indeed surprising. Here are some of the most interesting points. First, "you are always sending a message." Think carefully about every word you say, even to so-called close friends and team members. Be consistent and disciplined in your message. You might even maintain a daily diary to ensure you are sending a consistent message. Avoid off-the-cuff comments and remarks, and never allow your emotions to speak. Always remember, it is better to listen and learn. Finally, do not personalize anything.

Good advice for CEOs can be found in the author Frank Outlaw's statement: "Watch your thoughts, they become words; watch your words, they become actions; watch your actions, they become habits; watch your habits, they become character; watch your character, for it becomes your destiny."[44]

A second surprise from the *Harvard Business Review* article is how much filtered information CEOs receive—some of it intentionally filtered. Most new CEOs make the mistake of thinking that they will be able to learn everything that is going on in the organization (including the good news and the bad) just because they are in charge. So how do you overcome this critical information problem? Here are a few suggestions:

» Hold weekly group meetings with all of your direct reports. Keep the meetings short and focused. Control the agenda and hold people accountable and responsible.

» Create an environment where no one is afraid to speak the truth. This is covered in detail in chapter 5, "Learning Entity," and chapter 8, "Distinctive Culture."

» Travel and engage with frontline employees. Visit unannounced and ask the right questions.

» Implement appropriate mechanisms that provide critical and timely information. Conduct town-hall meetings and breakfast or lunch meetings.

One tool I found effective for information-sharing is what I called "Coffee with the Chairman." The formal method of this meeting gathered everyone in the office for coffee and a light snack. After some brief remarks, I mingled with employees to determine what was on their mind. The informal meetings consisted of inviting new and existing executives to have coffee outside the office. These are good ways for the CEO to assess key talent in a less formal setting, and it's a wonderful opportunity to get answers to direct questions about the organization or its strategy. Some CEOs take this a step further by inviting key executives to a one-on-one dinner, either at a restaurant or at the leader's home.

7. Make Safety a Top Priority and a Core Value

Make safety a core value and embed it in the company culture. Just as a code of conduct is established for integrity and personal behavior, safety deserves an equal position in the organization. Any violation of the safety code of conduct should be dealt with as seriously and as forcefully as integrity violations. Leaders have a responsibility to ensure that all employees go home to their families in the same condition that they arrived for work. Create an environment in which employees have the confidence, integrity, and strength to admit when something has gone wrong and then take corrective action immediately.

8. Determine Where True Economic Value Is Created

Measure each executive for value-creation contribution. In a highly dynamic and unstable business world, it is easy to get distracted and lose sight of this essential element in any business. Jim Collins explores this in his book *Good to Great* when he wonders "what drives your economic engine" and offers the format of a numerator and denominator as a formula to answer the question. Each business needs to be evaluated this way, and don't underestimate what it will take to get the right answer. Here's an example from my own career.

One of our business units was driven mainly by engineering hours. Since Economic Value Added (EVA™) was a core value of the company, it was natural to use economic value created as the logical numerator. Since the business was driven by engineering hours, it was natural to use these hours as the denominator. The net result of this was the economic value created per engineering hour. By assigning an economic value to each engineering hour, the organization became more focused on the importance of how time was spent and the impact that each hour had on the overall performance of the company.

The value-creation concept applies to individuals as well. It is important to get everyone in the organization thinking about how he or she impacts value and how it can be measured. If possible, develop key metrics for each executive. Although this is more difficult to measure for some positions, you should require each of your direct reports to provide an answer to this question as part of an annual or semiannual appraisal process. This needs to be both a qualitative and a quantitative assessment.

I always lived by this rule: at the end of the day I would ask myself, what value did I create today? Ask yourself this question and be honest, and encourage others to be honest as well, since a truthful answer can open up some very interesting dialogue. A former close senior colleague had an exemplary perspective on value creation. He always viewed the first duty of the legal department where he was chief counsel to be value protection in the form of sound contracts, accurate disclosure, legal compliance, and fending off plaintiffs. His belief was that the value of the enterprise was composed of existing value plus value added; losing the former would sink a company more quickly than losing the latter. This is sage advice.

9. Develop a Robust Sales Cadence, Backlog, and Forecasting System

As a new CEO, you must have the ability to forecast accurately. A sales-cadence process that allows you to see the flow of orders and backlog is essential. Every business is different, but you should be able to implement some system that captures orders and backlog. This information needs to be captured in a timely fashion along with the respective estimated profitability (at least on a gross margin basis).

In addition to the sales-cadence process, a CEO needs a strong forecasting system that provides an outlook over the coming twelve months. The forecasting system must be grounded in reality and based on facts, economic models, history, trends, and at times even science. Emotion and gut feelings cannot be the major drivers of the forecasting system. Since the CEO's credibility is on the line with the investment community and the board, don't underestimate the system's importance. Pay close attention to key economic drivers and analysts' estimates and ensure that you are getting truthful and unfiltered information from your internal sources. In order to strengthen the process, a CEO should seriously consider adding an in-house economist to the team to standardize economic models and data used to assess risk.

In the book *The Black Swan*, Nassim Nicholas Taleb discusses forecasting in considerable detail. He states that "forecasting without incorporating an error rate uncovers three fallacies, all arising from the same misconception about the nature of uncertainty." His three fallacies include variability matters, failing to take into account forecast degradation as the projected period lengthens, and misunderstanding the random character of the variables being forecast. After a detailed discussion on these three fallacies, he makes the following powerful statement: "Even if you agree with a given forecast, you have to worry about the real possibility of significant divergence from it."[45]

You might argue that this precarious situation is easily avoided simply by not providing earnings guidance, other than perhaps for the current quarter. If a CEO has a fairly accurate forecasting system and the business is predictable and not subject to remarkable volatility, then an argument can be made for providing earnings guidance. If, however, the forecasting system has been unreliable and the business is highly cyclical and subject to considerable volatility, a strong argument can be made for not providing earnings guidance. This is an important decision that a CEO needs to discuss with the board. The major risk of this strategy is that it plays into the hands of sell-side analysts with possible unintended consequences, such as higher earnings targets because of unrealistic expectations.

10. Bring the Global Leadership Team Together

A newly appointed leader needs to gather the leadership team early so that they clearly understand the strategy and direction of the enterprise. It is also important for the team members to hear about expectations directly from their new leader. The leader needs to explain to the team the targets, the metrics, and the three key focus areas of the organization as it moves forward.

The first week that I was officially CEO at the beginning of 2008, I assembled the entire global leadership team so that they could hear directly from me about the strategies and challenges of the company. The meeting provided an excellent opportunity to not only address questions but also motivate and unify the team.

The Specifics: Actions After One Year

By serving on a board, you will gain a different perspective, which is critical for your development. Also, you increase your chances of getting other board seats later in your career, particularly if your CEO tenure is shorter than you planned. Board membership is also a personal lifeline and an effective way to stay engaged with the broader leadership community.

With the involvement of your CHRO, conduct a 360 review of the team including yourself. This feedback is highly important to a new CEO. Use this information along with your first annual report card from the board to reflect on the year. At a minimum, take several days and go somewhere to truly reflect and focus on the past year so that you can make any necessary adjustments in the year to come. This is discussed in chapter 5, "Learning Entity."

Finally, sit down with the lead director, the chairman of the management development and compensation committee, and the chairman of the corporate governance and nominating committee and have an honest and open dialogue about your performance. Constructive feedback is essential. At the end of the dialogue session, there should be complete alignment with respect to any specified actions and goals.

Takeaways

Leadership tenure today is ephemeral. In order for leaders to increase their probability of a longer tenure, they must follow a solid recipe that includes specific elements for success through proactive actions.

The main recipe takeaways from this chapter include the following points:

» A proactive mind-set is key to success.

» Build an appropriate number of lifelines through proactive actions as antidotes to potential bad-luck events in the future.

» Create a comprehensive road-map list of proactive actions that must be developed.

» Focus on learning and continuous self-improvement.

» When assuming a new leadership position, first actions are vital.

» Implementing the ten critical actions of new CEOs is most important.

» Follow up and assess specific actions after one year.

PART 2

The Six Practices of a Healthy Enterprise

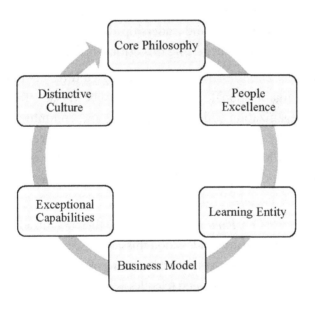

Part 2 is a guidebook and a framework for leaders who are working to build an enduring organization that performs at a high level irrespective of economic cycles. Here is a summary of each chapter:

» *Chapter 4: Business Model.* The most complex task of leadership is finding and implementing the right business model. This chapter outlines how to decide on and implement a successful and innovative model.

» *Chapter 5: Learning Entity.* Companies must learn from both success and failure, and doing that requires a unique combination of efficient corporate mechanisms and processes and a healthy organizational culture. Lessons learned are the cornerstone of building a learning entity. This chapter outlines the top thirty lessons I learned, both inside and outside the company, as a CEO.

» *Chapter 6: Exceptional Capabilities.* Strong operational capabilities and their consistent execution increase the potential for value creation and sustainable competitive advantage. This chapter outlines twenty of these must-have exceptional capabilities.

» *Chapter 7: People Excellence.* Building an exceptional team is vital to success but is nearly impossible to do without powerful internal talent-management and leadership-development processes. This chapter is all about getting this critical task right.

» *Chapter 8: Distinctive Culture.* Strong cultures are built on five core organizational elements that must be in place. These include an organization-wide understanding and commitment to core company values; a critical number of employees whose own values allow for sharing this core value connection; a strong and consistently implemented business model; a values-based leader at the top; and effective mechanisms.

» *Chapter 9: Core Philosophy.* Leaders and their organizations must be aligned to a clearly understood mission statement and core values. This chapter discusses the implications of consistently living out a company's core values and relentlessly adhering to the core mission.

Reaching the Highest Summit in a Business Enterprise

Viewing the journey of a business through the lens of mountaineering brings vividly to life the thrill of success and the challenges of failure. In the book *Extreme Alpinism: Climbing Light, Fast, and High*, authors Mark Twight and James Martin capture brightly one of the key metaphors used in this book concerning the essential lifelines needed for an ascent to the summit: "Alpine climbing is unsafe and no rationalization can change that. It's a game of survival. Dying, or even getting hurt, means you lost."[46]

The same principle applies to business. In our hypercompetitive and rapidly changing global economy, enterprises face unprecedented competition that is made even more difficult by an unstable economic landscape. Still, the survival of the company is paramount, and one misstep can lead to the spectacular failure of individual leaders, the organizations they lead, or both.

Leaders must fully cultivate their lifelines to enhance their luck spread and keep their career (and perhaps their organization) alive. In *Extreme Alpinism*, the principle factors that appear on a climber's "radar" when facing a climb include safety, speed, maturity, vigilance, acclimation, self-rescue and first aid, and death and survival. However, the wild card of luck can never be taken lightly, and the best climbers know that they must never take anything for granted. The parallel between a climber's radar list and the radar list of a business leader is striking and important enough to offer a quick side-by-side comparison:

» *Speed.* For climbers, speed means "less time exposed to danger." In business, speed equates to cycle time that is measured by how long it takes to execute a task successfully. It also includes how long it takes to get innovation to the marketplace and deliver a product to the customer, integrate an acquisition, or start up a new site. Speed enhances an enterprise's safety by lowering costs and increasing its ability to capture market share.

» *Maturity.* For mountaineers, maturity means a holistic integration of everything they know that goes beyond even technical skill and ambition. In the business world, this means having precocious leadership characteristics underpinned by sound judgment, common sense, and a realistic assessment of facts. Maturity also is what guides the successful collaboration of a seasoned leader and a strong board of directors.

» *Vigilance.* Climbers do not expose themselves to life-threatening situations as they ascend to the summit. They diligently use their innate senses, judgment, training, and experience at all times. Visionary business leaders are no different. They are vigilant during the ascent to the summit, and they use all of their precocious characteristics to guide the team and the organization. They implement appropriate mechanisms that provide critical information, and they use their senses to detect changes in end-markets, the macroeconomic environment, and competitors in order to avoid potentially catastrophic traps.

» *Acclimation.* Climbers take the time to adjust to increasing altitude by bivouacking along the way to allow the body to adjust naturally to higher altitudes. Mountaineers also prepare themselves to face the challenge with the lifelines provided by specialized medicine and oxygen. Enterprises and leaders must also prepare every day for the summit. That means implementing the nine lifelines outlined in this book. It means taking proactive actions to ensure that an abundant number of lifelines are created along the way to ensure a safe ascent to the summit.

» *Self-rescue and first aid.* For climbers, expertise in self-rescue techniques and first aid can be the difference between life and death. Building an appropriate number of lifelines is a leader's form of self-rescue. For an organization or enterprise, an injury that requires first aid might be the loss of a major customer, a lawsuit, a new competitor, or a significant increase in the cost of a base raw material. Both a leader and his or her enterprise must have the ability to recover and resume the journey.

» *Death and survival.* Mountaineers know the threat of death is real. The threat of death in business might mean becoming irrelevant or worse, through an unwanted takeover, a merger, or a bankruptcy. This threat is very real. For example, only approximately 10 percent of the Fortune 500 companies that were on the original 1955 list remain today. Admittedly, some of the companies that disappeared from the list have gone private, but the fact that almost 90 percent of the original 500 have disappeared is an astounding number!

CHAPTER 4

Business Model

I discovered that the best innovation is sometimes the
company, the way you organize a company.
—Steve Jobs[47]

Only a small number of companies will actually become great. It is no different in mountain climbing, where only a handful of individuals are rated as extraordinarily gifted high-altitude climbers. This is simply the reality of the world. But it doesn't mean that the other companies and other climbers cannot achieve some form of excellence and be highly successful.

Irrespective of whether a company or a climber achieves elite status, the ultimate goal is to continuously improve. The path to the ultimate summit of greatness for an enterprise begins with implementing an innovative business model, a step that can significantly improve a company's chance to achieve elite status.

The most difficult and complex part of a value-creation equation—which ultimately determines greatness for any enterprise—is choosing an innovative business model and connecting it to a stated and followed mission statement. (See chapter 9, "Core Philosophy.") Although all nine lifelines outlined here are equally important in building an elite organization, leaders must understand that the mission of the company is ultimately manifested through the business model.

The business model must be designed in an innovative way so that it provides the enterprise with a competitive and sustainable advantage. An innovative business model must allow each business unit or platform to operate efficiently and effectively, be designed and tailored to the specifics of the enterprise, and offer scalability at the lowest cost possible.

Getting the business model correct is no easy undertaking, but the rewards can be substantial. Steve Jobs at Apple knew this well. As quoted in Walter Isaacson's biography *Steve Jobs*, he said, "I discovered that the best innovation is sometimes the company, the way you organize a company." It is not a surprise that Jobs paid so much attention to the business model. This is an insightful perspective that the way the company is organized and functions can be the ultimate innovation.

Every leader needs to have total clarity and focus on his or her chosen business model and realize that it might take a considerable amount of time and effort to get it right. The right business model includes two vital and interdependent components: the *recipe* and the *organizational structure*. The recipe represents all the critical and unique practices that define the company, and the organizational structure is used to execute these practices in the most effective and efficient way as possible.

The Recipe

A good place to start in better understanding the recipe is Jim Collins's book *Great by Choice*. He defines the recipe as "a set of durable operating practices that create a replicable and consistent success formula; it is clear and concrete, enabling the entire enterprise to unify and organize its efforts, giving clear guidance regarding what to do and what not to do."[48] Michael Porter refers to this recipe as "Unique Activities" in his insightful article "What Is Strategy?" when he states that "competitive strategy is about being different. It means deliberately choosing a different set of activities to deliver a unique mix of value."[49]

Both Porter and Collins use Southwest Airlines as an example of a company that got the recipe right. Porter cites Southwest's unique activities, such as not offering meals or providing assigned seats and standardizing its airplane fleet on the Boeing 737, as ways the airline "staked out a unique and valuable strategic position based on a tailored set of activities." Collins cites Southwest's decision to remain a short-haul carrier, utilize the 737 as its primary aircraft, focus on the passenger, and avoid food service as some of ten critical elements underpinning its success. For other organizations that have managed to get the recipe right, Porter and Collins cite IKEA and Progressive Insurance, respectively.

Successful mountaineers also use a recipe-like, step-by-step process they trust will keep them safe, which includes physical training, mental preparation, planning, and equipment, according to the book *Alpine Climbing: Techniques to Take You Higher* by authors Mark Houston and Kathy Cosley.[50] As demonstrated by the Southwest Airlines story, leaders must take the time to search out the unique recipe that defines their organization. Is it possible to articulate ten unique practices that define your organization and its current position in the market? I believe that in order to successfully define the recipe of an organization, the ideal number of identified unique practices needs to be in a range of six to ten. Later, in chapter 9 in this book, "Core Philosophy," I'll introduce an innovative process that IBM used to develop its core values that could help in this recipe-creation process. No matter how you derive your answer, you'll have to complete this first step before embarking on the second element of the business model, the organizational structure.

Example of a Highly Successful Recipe

A powerful example of a successful recipe that I have discovered in my research is the one developed by Roper, a diversified growth company based in Florida. Roper provides engineered products and solutions that create global leadership positions across a diverse set of niche markets, including software information networks, medical, water, energy, and transportation. Roper is also discussed in chapter 8 in this book, "Distinctive Culture." Roper's 2010 Annual Report to Shareholders stated the following:

Our performance will continue to be driven by the simple ideas that have transformed the enterprise over the prior decade—focusing on cash return disciplines, seeking and maintaining leadership positions in niche markets, generating high gross margins, developing outstanding operational teams, delivering compelling cash flow using our asset-light business model, deploying capital to drive internal growth, and continuing to acquire new businesses with great growth prospect.[51]

These points continued to be highlighted in the 2011 and 2012 annual reports, along with some additional salient items. In essence, what Roper has articulated in its public statements is its recipe. I would identify the unique activities that make up Roper's recipe as follows:

» cash return discipline that delivers compelling free cash flow

» niche-market leadership positions through a diverse set of businesses

» focus on proprietary and differentiated solutions that generate high gross margins

» exceptional operating managers who are accountable

» a nimble governance system

» asset-light businesses, minimal capital expenditures, and efficient working capital

» effective and efficient redeployment of free cash flow to drive growth

» strong growth prospects for acquisitions

Roper's recipe, which I believe is made up of the above eight elements, is probably the reason that the company has posted superior results. This is clearly an extraordinary recipe that can be used as a model on how to develop a recipe for your business.

Organizational Structure of the Enterprise

Organizational structure is the second element of an enterprise's business model. At a very high level, there are three major models (and of course many variations) leaders can use to structure how an organization operates: the decentralized model, the hybrid model, and the centralized model.

Enterprises using a *decentralized* business model are usually organized so that business units operate independently as essentially stand-alone businesses. Organizations using a *hybrid* (or matrix) model are built around a matrix system, with the functional heads responsible for their teams globally. For example, the enterprise CFO is responsible for all finance functions across the company. Under this structure, the business unit CFOs report directly to the enterprise leader, but they must also function as business partners at the local level. Then there is the *centralized* model that is also referred to as the integrated enterprise. In the centralized model, the entire enterprise is set up as one cohesive and integrated unit that operates as a whole.

Of course, each model must be underpinned by well-designed and efficient systems and processes and a framework that allows an enterprise to execute its mission flawlessly, without the bureaucratic policies that normally slow or cripple an organization.

Decentralized Business Model

Successful enterprises that operate using the decentralized model must have a powerful entrepreneurial culture, strong enterprise controls, and business units that consistently post good operating results. Another important condition of the decentralized business model is a steady, noncyclical end-markets business environment. Under this model you may find the position of president and/or chief operating officer.

Stability is important for this model, since the cost structure is usually higher than either the hybrid or centralized models. For example, the structure usually includes a global headquarters, regional headquarters, and sometimes multiple headquarters within a country since each business platform operates independently.

Hybrid or Matrix Model

Hybrid organizations must have a team of strong and talented functional leaders—including top financial, information-technology, and human-resources officers—and all these leaders must possess many of the thirty precocious characteristics outlined in this book. Trust and teamwork are vitally important to a hybrid enterprise, as is exceptional operational capabilities—like the Lean continuous-improvement discipline, shared global services, and integrated supply-chain management—so that scale benefits are globally captured.

Since the structure reduces the need for regional business headquarters, these facilities are usually eliminated or significantly reduced. This model is appropriate for both nonhomogeneous and homogeneous businesses (multiple or single business platform) and requires that the company operate in an entrepreneurial and proactive manner as well.

Centralized or Fully Integrated Enterprise Model

On the surface, the highly centralized model is compelling from a cost-savings and efficiency standpoint. Our business-model search at Harsco led me to the door of two Fortune 100 companies that operated under this model, and our due diligence revealed the fully integrated business model worked beautifully for them and the savings that they demonstrated were immense.

I also researched Apple, a strong example of a successful integrated enterprise model. In the book *Steve Jobs*, author Walter Isaacson talks about the significance of the business model to Apple, writing that Jobs "did not organize Apple into semiautonomous divisions; he closely controlled all his teams and he pushed them to work as one cohesive and flexible company, with one profit-and-loss bottom line."[52]

Still, enterprises considering this model must ensure that they have a modern and fully integrated information technology (IT) infrastructure using one enterprise-resource planning (ERP) system. The cost of implementing a standardized global ERP and IT infrastructure can be cost-prohibitive, time-prohibitive, and simply unrealistic for many companies. Secondly, for the centralized model to work well, a homogeneous business enterprise is preferable to several different and distinct business platforms.

Organizational Structure Conclusions

My own analysis of the different organizational structures revealed a not too surprising truth: there is no perfect or magical operating structure. There is almost an endless number of organizational structures that can be adopted, but no two operating structures are identical. What is important is to use the model that fits the enterprise-specific recipe and the culture of the company, the markets served, and the operating style of the company.

Results of an Effective and Innovative Business Model

So what are the results of focusing on choosing an effective and innovative business model? First, companies that solve the value-creation equation by getting both their specific enterprise recipe and organizational structure right should generate superior returns due to the clear, sustainable, competitive advantage they can ultimately create. An exceptional business model should manifest some very strong characteristics. Based on my long business career, my studies of elite companies, and many discussions with other CEOs, I have identified certain superior characteristics that are usually manifested by an enterprise with an exceptional business model. Enterprises that posses an innovative business model will usually manifest many or most of the following characteristics:

- » high gross margins
- » recurring, predictable revenue streams
- » strong operating margins
- » high return on invested capital
- » prodigious operating and free cash flows
- » minimal capital expenditures
- » effective redeployment of capital

Underpinning these strong operating metrics, these exceptional companies usually have certain other characteristics like niche market positions, recession-proof market, stable market cycles, high barriers to entry, superior technology, and innovation capabilities.

Characteristics of Successful Business Models

Here are more of the major characteristics of the most successful business models:

» *High gross margins.* Businesses need to generate prodigious gross margins between 30 and 40 percent, but businesses that generate between 40 and 50 percent are most likely operating with a superior business model. In 2012, Apple had gross margins of 44 percent and Roper posted an incredible 56 percent gross margin. As a point of reference, the average gross margin for the S&P 500 Industrials is in the lower ranges of 30 percent.

» *Recurring, predictable revenue streams.* The ability to forecast accurately because of less volatility in results affords an enterprise the luxury of planning for the long-term. Recurring revenues, particularly when coupled with less cyclical end-markets, usually translate to predictable earnings and cash flow.

» *Strong operating margins.* Generating superior returns on invested capital requires strong operating margins. I believe that operating margins after all cost allocations are included should be at least double-digit, around 10 percent or better, to ensure an enterprise achieves an adequate return on invested capital. Of course, outliers exist with respect to superior operating margins. Apple posted an incredible 36 percent in 2012, while Roper posted an impressive 26 percent. Strong operating margins are necessary because many organizations have a cost of capital of around 9 to 10 percent, and in some cases even higher. That's why the return on invested capital needs to at least equal the cost of capital so that shareholder value is not destroyed. Superior businesses have return on invested capital characteristics of mid to upper teens.

» *Prodigious operating and free cash flows.* The lifeline of every organization begins with strong cash flow from operations, but ultimately it's the free-cash-flow number that is most important. Free cash flow is calculated directly from the company's cash-flow statement, starting with cash flow from operations less capital expenditures less dividends. Since free cash flow is not a defined term under generally accepted accounting principles, the definition will vary due to several variables, including dividends and the two components of capital expenditures.

The most traditional method of calculating free cash flow is to take cash flow from operations less capital expenditures. This means that dividends are excluded from the calculation. There are instances when dividends should be deducted in calculating the free-cash-flow number. To me, the dividends number should be deducted in the free-cash-flow calculation if the company has a long history of paying dividends and if it has shown a consistent pattern of increasing the dividend. When this is the case, the dividend is not really discretionary because there would be negative ramifications to the company's stock price if the dividend was stopped or reduced significantly. In cases where the dividend has a notable discretionary element to it, it should then be excluded from the free-cash-flow calculation.

Another complexity to calculating free cash flow are the two components of capital expenditures: maintenance and growth capital. There are enterprises that have organic growth opportunities, so they invest considerably in growth capital expenditures, where the maintenance capital is required to sustain the current revenue streams of the business. Thus, it is helpful to break out and understand these two components of capital expenditures, because the growth capital has a certain discretionary element to it.

Although it is helpful to know these two components, the free-cash-flow calculation should stand as defined above (all capital expenditures included). No matter how the dividend is treated, what is important is to arrive at the true free cash available to the company. The free or discretionary cash is the capital available to invest in growth, including acquisitions, paying down debt, repurchasing shares, or increasing the dividend further.

» *Minimal capital expenditures.* The best businesses are usually ones that require a minimal amount of capital expenditures but have a strong element of technology and knowledge-based solutions. On the other hand, there are some businesses that require significant investment in capital expenditures. This is usually in the form of both maintenance capital (to sustain the current revenue stream) and growth capital (organic initiatives to grow revenues). As explained in chapter 6 in this book, "Exceptional Capabilities," these businesses need to ensure that they perform at the top tier of their group relative to capital efficiency.

» *Efficient redeployment of capital.* Businesses that redeploy their free or discretionary cash flow effectively and efficiently usually create substantial shareholder value. Return on invested capital, sales per dollar of growth capital expenditures, cash return on invested capital, and return on equity are some of the ways to measure this business effectiveness, including EVA (which is discussed in chapter 5, "Learning Entity").

Effective Business Model Framework

A high-level view of an innovative business model framework is depicted in the chart:

<table>
<tr><td colspan="3" align="center">

Innovative Business Model Framework

</td></tr>
<tr>
<td>Recipe: Identify all the critical practices that define and are unique to the enterprise, 6 to 10. Keep it simple and engage the organization in identifying them.</td>
<td>Organizational Structure:* Three broad models include: centralized, decentralized and hybrid. The centralized is a fully integrated enterprise. In the decentralized model, the business units are independent. The hybrid model operates under a matrix system.</td>
<td>Effective Business Model Characteristics: high gross margins, high operating margins, high ROIC, prodigious free cash flow, recurring and predictable revenue streams, minimal capital expenditures, and effective employment of cash.</td>
</tr>
</table>

Organizational Structure - Additional points summarized in chart below:

1. Centralized or fully integregated model.	• This model works with these characteristics: a homogeneous business; standardized and integrated information technology platform (one ERP); strong organizational skills; and, standard global processes.
2. Decentralized model.	• This model works with these characteristics: strong entrepreneurial culture; effective enterprise controls; consistent high performer; multiple business platforms (non-homogeneous); and, majority of business is not exposed to highly cyclical markets.
3. Hybrid or matrix model.	• This model works with these characteristics: strong and talented functional leaders; standard processes; multiple business platforms (non-homogeneous) or single platform (homogeneous); high level of trust and teamwork; exceptional capabilities such as global services; and, operates as an entrepreneurial and proactive enterprise .

Takeaways

Choosing a business model is the most difficult and complex part of a value-creation equation that a leader needs to solve. With a solid foundation built on the other lifelines discussed in the book, the business model should provide the enterprise with a competitive and sustainable advantage. Getting this right puts an enterprise on the path to excellence through substantial, long-term value creation.

The two interdependent elements to a high-performing and innovative business model are the recipe and the organizational structure. Enterprises that get these two elements right usually manifest many of the following strong performance characteristics: high gross margins; recurring, predictable revenue streams; high operating margins; high return on invested capital; prodigious cash flows; minimal capital expenditures; and effective redeployment of free cash flow.

CHAPTER 5

Learning Entity

*Success does not consist in never making mistakes but
in never making the same one a second time.*
—*George Bernard Shaw*[53]

Enterprises need to learn constructive lessons from both their own mistakes and those of others, and they must take appropriate measures to ensure that the mistakes are not repeated. Mark Houston and Kathy Cosley illustrate this concept well in the book *Alpine Climbing: Techniques to Take You Higher*. Their sage advice on learning from both types of experiences should be taken to heart by leaders:

> While personal experience in the mountains is ultimately the best teacher, you can also benefit from watching other climbers in action. Listen to their stories … and try to imagine what you would do in various situations. Read about accidents and analyze them. When analyzing another party's accident or response to a risky situation, put yourself in their place. Try to see what factors brought on the risk and whether

or not they were foreseeable in that situation. Imagine alternative actions they might have taken to better manage the risk.[54]

The focus of this chapter is on understanding the five key elements necessary to create a learning entity and on sharing the top thirty lessons that I learned (both inside and outside the company) during my career. These key leadership lessons reflect my own approach to building an organization that truly understands why learning from experience is so vital to its long-term survival. As President John F. Kennedy once said, "Leadership and learning are indispensable to each other."[55] These thirty lessons learned (negative and positive) coalesce around an enterprise's mechanisms, processes, and culture and are supported by a large body of work that has been published over the years about creating and building a learning organization.

However, before examining both the learning-entity elements and the lessons learned, let's briefly reconnect once more with the principal climbing metaphor that underpins the concepts in this book. Mountaineering authors Mark F. Twight and James Martin provide easily transferable advice that seems tailor-made for organizations and their leaders in their book *Extreme Alpinism: Climbing Light, Fast, and High*:

> Experience acts as a shield against disaster. An experienced climber spots potential problems and takes the right steps to avoid them. Experience provides the raw material for imagining hard routes in the mountains ... Learn how to learn. Write everything down ... Read the stories of the grand masters of alpinism ... And learn from your mistakes. The intelligent climber makes each mistake only once, and he is cured.[56]

This is advice that enterprises can surely benefit from in today's competitive global environment.

Learning Entity Essential Elements

An enterprise must implement an appropriate number of mechanisms in order to ensure that it learns valuable and actionable lessons from both success and failure. Five effective mechanisms are the key-seats executive retreat, an internal university, the postevent debrief, a learning committee, and joint ventures/strategic alliances. These mechanisms need to be underpinned by a vigorous process and a strong culture. Culture and process are explored in chapter 8, "Distinctive Culture," and chapter 4, "Business Model."

The *executive retreat* is the forum where lessons learned can be shared and dialogued with the leaders of the organization. This is the group that will implement the necessary changes for failures and will also be responsible for adopting winning strategies. This is the group that the CEO will ultimately hold accountable for results.

An *internal university* can take many forms. Most organizations do not have the vast resources to create a best-of-class learning center. The good news is that with minimal resources and the smart use of a vast array of technological resources and case studies, all enterprises can create an effective learning-entity environment. The internal university should be supplemented with outside training, particularly focused development at prestigious institutions.

The *postevent debrief* is a formal process established by the enterprise where all key initiatives are thoroughly and completely reviewed with the sole objective of learning. The debrief needs to occur for both negative and positive outcomes with the objective of learning and improving. Honesty and transparency must underpin the assessment and the proposed actions.

A *learning committee* should be formed in the organization, and it should function as a focal point for supporting employee learning in accordance with the company's mission statement and core values. Learning committees are highly effective in academia, and I believe that a well-focused committee in a business enterprise can be just as competent.

Joint ventures and *strategic alliances* can be powerful forces in supporting a learning entity. There is so much that can be learned from partners. Different and innovative business models, exceptional capabilities, people excellence, and other lifelines can be discovered through strong partners.

CEO Lessons Learned: Top Thirty

The thirty lessons that follow are segmented by major category. They reflect the lessons I learned about creating a learning entity directly from my role as Harsco chairman, president, and CEO, as well as knowledge I have gained from almost four decades of business experience. As the author Minna Antrim put it, "Experience is a good teacher, but she sends in terrific bills."[57] How true! My goal here is to minimize the bills that come due for current and future CEOs and business leaders. If you are one of these leaders or expect to be, think of these as my lifeline to you. All the lessons learned have the benefit of perfect hindsight and they should be viewed in that light.

Lessons Learned: Personal Characteristics

1. Don't Discount Your Instinct—Go With It

During the course of my tenure as CEO, there were some instances in which my initial instinct was absolutely correct, and yet I failed to trust what it was telling me. Every time I did this, I regretted it and I paid a price. Some of the lessons learned in this chapter are a result of not listening to this so-called "sixth sense."

Over the years, I have discussed the subject of instincts with several leaders, and they also echoed the point about regrets over not following through on their instincts. Most CEOs and successful business leaders have an uncanny ability to sense or *see* the right answer or business direction, even when logic, research, or even a CFO's return-on-investment calculation said otherwise. Instinct is part of your precocious leadership skill set, so use it wisely. A couple of key areas where instinct is essential to the success of a leader is when difficult people decisions need to be made and when choosing which strategic projects to pursue and which to stop doing.

2. Don't Assume That Everyone Will Be Like You

When I was appointed CEO, my predecessor gave me some wonderful hiring advice in the form of a compliment. He said that if everyone who works for me in the future serves me the way I served him, he had no doubt that I'd be an enormous success.

I mistakenly assumed that everyone would perform like I did and have similar priorities, competence, and loyalty. The lesson learned here is, don't view the world and others through the prism of your values, your discipline, and your abilities. Just because you may have delivered results your entire career, don't automatically expect others to perform at the same level for you.

3. Remember, It's Not Your Job to Make Friends

Seeing the world through the eyes of the CEO is much different from, say, the CFO or COO. Being promoted internally is dramatically different from being an external hire, and it needs the right mind-set. Accept the fact that you probably will not have many real friends once you reach the top position. Organizational relationships are highly complex when you are a CEO. Don't make them more complex by trying to make or win friends. You can be empathetic, but don't confuse that with friendship. The world is transactional, and unfortunately you need to be skeptical about people's intentions when you are a CEO. Clearly there are exceptions, but you are much better off to assume every other outcome is rare.

4. Be Proactive in Protecting Your Position and Reputation

The CEO's tenure is fleeting when measured against the backdrop of a long-established organization. Don't make yours shorter by being passive. Remember what Winston Churchill once said: "Men occasionally stumble over the truth, but most of them pick themselves up and hurry off as if nothing happened."[58] Churchill certainly captured the reality of the CEO's life, the enormity of the job and the attendant responsibilities. Remember that as the leader, you are ultimately accountable and responsible for everything that happens on your watch. In the end, you are left alone to face the consequences when there is a cacophony of voices that are unhappy about the stock price, so protect yourself by building as many lifelines as possible.

Let's briefly review specific measures that a leader should take to protect his reputation and position. First, the leader needs to be proactive by implementing the recommendations in chapter 3, "Proactive Actions." Second, a leader needs to study and clearly understand the lessons learned in this chapter and ones that are shared by other leaders, such as Jack Welch (former CEO of GE). And finally, a leader needs to understand that the more lifelines that are built, the better his chances for success and a long tenure.

5. Treat All People Equally and with Respect

Not all lessons learned need to be negative. I have always tried to treat everyone with respect, no matter their position in the organization. I worked hard, strove to exemplify the highest integrity, and was loyal. Many people have commented to me over the years that I had a nice way about me and that I was good with people. This behavior came naturally to me. Because of the way I treated people over the years, I developed a large group of professional contacts that proved to be of enormous value when I left Harsco. I was surprised that I had unintentionally developed a vast and valuable network that provided support and opportunities after I left my position as CEO. I count this network as a true treasure of personal lifelines. The lesson here is to treat everyone the way you would want to be treated. In the end, it's a much more valuable legacy than even the position you once held.

6. Allow for a Period of Inner Reflection and Growth

As discussed in the preface, no matter what happens in the organization, the ultimate responsibility always resides with the CEO. It's a real no-excuse job! That is why a CEO must set aside time, at least annually, for inner reflection and growth away from both the office and home. The time and place is not as important as the consistent practice, so set aside a week and stick to the habit. Out of that inner reflection, perspective should be gained and decisions should be made.

As for personal growth, I recommend that the CEO regularly attend outside training sessions or conduct visits with another business to benchmark practices. You might consider asking for an up-close visit to the company where you are on the board, or even tapping into your network of bankers and colleagues (at associations or professional groups) for recommendations of places to visit.

Lessons Learned: People Excellence

7. Get an A-Player for the Chief Human-Resources Officer

The selection of a seasoned and experienced chief human-resources officer (CHRO) is a key decision for every leader (discussed in more detail in chapter 3, "Proactive Actions"). At the beginning of my tenure as Harsco CEO, we had in place an extremely competent and talented internal senior officer who functioned also as the CHRO. The individual was not a career HR professional, and the global HR function was not the executive's full-time focus. My instinct told me that I needed a full-time individual with the necessary background, training, and experience to oversee the global human-resources function. Yet, as clear as the right decision seems to be in hindsight, I decided to stay with the status quo for another year.

When I finally decided to make a change, the search for the right individual unfortunately took almost two years and was conducted right in the middle of a worsening global economic crisis. Bad luck was a major factor in our search, as two top candidates ultimately declined the job because of more lucrative opportunities with larger organizations. As a result of not having a seasoned CHRO on the team, I spent a considerable amount of my time recruiting, developing, and retaining key personnel and was deprived of another set of highly experienced eyes to help me evaluate leadership-team recruits from outside the company and provide advice and insight during our strategic business-transformation process.

8. Promote from Within, and Limit Senior-Management-Level Outside Hires

All high-performing companies have successful processes for developing talent from within. My experience at Harsco bears this out. However, because of accelerated growth, we made a determination that we needed to augment our talent-management and leadership-development process with outside hires. This resulted in the recruitment of about twelve positions of our key seats from outside the company. The results were less than stellar. About a quarter of these new hires did not pan out, and among those who stayed, the outside hires were more expensive and generally less able to fit in with the culture.

The lesson here is that external hires have the potential to create a number of problems, including disrupting internal compensation schemes, negatively impacting culture, harming company morale, and reducing feelings of company loyalty and connection. Genuinely excellent people usually do not leave good companies, so the odds of finding a true A-player from the outside who is aligned with your organization's culture and values are small. That's why you should take every opportunity to hire from the inside, even when the ideal skill set is less than perfect. In one particular case, we took a considerable risk with one individual, and he surprised everyone with an exceptionally strong performance. Give high-potential individuals a chance; provide them with stretch assignments. You may be pleasantly surprised.

However, if you must look externally, increase your chances by following some of these basic rules. First, with the assistance of the CHRO, implement a comprehensive interviewing process. Make sure that you have the perfect blend of backgrounds and positions represented on the team. Interviewing is more a process than a science, so it is imperative that the process is sound. (See chapter 7, "People Excellence," for the nine key interview characteristics.)

Consider having the top candidates prepare a formal presentation on how they would approach the job. You'll gain a different perspective on the applicants' abilities beyond the typical interview and assessment tools. Then, before making a final decision, you should do a comprehensive due-diligence that includes an exhaustive background and reference check. In addition to verifying financial, ethical, and legal information and status, interview current and former peers, subordinates, and supervisors of the candidate's current employer and talk with affiliated organizations who may know the individual well. Do not delegate this to the search firm.

Once new executives are hired, immerse them in an intensive onboarding program that is focused on the culture and values of the company. Moreover, provide constant—not annual or semiannual—feedback to new team members to give them the best chance to be effective.

9. Establish Appropriate Mechanisms to Embed and Assess People Characteristics

One of the important actions that we took at Harsco to develop our A-team was establishing a list of benchmark characteristics for all key-seats members, including new hires. While the idea of using these nine personal characteristics to measure the appropriateness of a potential key-seat member, as well as an existing member, was excellent, our lesson learned was in proper implementation and integration of the standard. Yes, these characteristics figured into our human-capital framework foundation, but they were not pushed strongly enough in existing internal processes. Our training materials and hiring process included these characteristics, but the effort lacked consistency.

In hindsight, had we implemented a nine-characteristics assessment that comprehensively measured and vetted each one, we could have possibly had different results. For example, some high-level individuals we thought met the characteristics fell short in at least one or more areas. From this experience, I learned the following three lessons:

» *Work with an outside HR specialist.* Hiring an external consultant, such as a corporate psychologist, to help in implementing a much more robust process for screening and assessing prospective candidates as well as existing employees could have possibly produced better results. The assessment process needs to ensure that the personal characteristics are fully embedded in the organization through appropriate mechanisms that have teeth.

» *Establish an efficient process.* As mentioned earlier, hiring is not a science, it's a process, so it is vital that the process be efficient and produce superior results consistently. This includes a complete and exhaustive process for checking a candidate's background and the validity of other candidate-provided information. For key senior positions, the CEO should personally be involved in the due-diligence process. For example, the CEO should contact the candidate's prior CEO or CEOs and have a candid dialogue.

» *Establish metrics to monitor the hiring and development process.* Create a reliable system to measure how well your hiring process and your internal talent development program is working and fix issues immediately.

10. Create a Winning Culture

Leaders must find a way to immunize the organization against the complacency, arrogance, and loss of discipline that may occur following success. The remedy to this debilitating situation is found in implementing a number of vital mechanisms, including all nine lifelines outlined in this book. Leaders must also make sure that the following specific mechanisms are in place:

» a well-defined core mission that everyone understands and is committed to

» core values that promote a culture of ethics and exceptional performance

» an entrepreneurial culture

» an innovation network and innovation culture

» pay linked to sustained value creation

» a way to hold people accountable for results

» functions and operating results benchmarked to world-class standards

» metrics and processes that provide insight and feedback on customer needs and market trends

» a best-of-class talent-management and leadership-development system that promotes excellence

» metrics and processes that provide insight and constructive feedback from employees

Lessons Learned: Transformation and Reinvention

11. Manage Change Well—Too Many Changes Are Highly Disruptive and Stressful

Harsco's transformation journey, which I initiated in 2008, was particularly complex and difficult. In addition to strengthening the management team, the transformation included launching three key strategic initiatives: *globalization* (emerging-markets expansion), *innovation* (new products and services), and *optimization* (significantly lowering the cost structure, including launching the OneHarsco initiative and developing new exceptional capabilities).

With perfect hindsight, we probably set the bar too high because of the perfect economic storm that we encountered. Hindsight reveals that we should have scaled back sooner a number of planned changes within each focus area, and we should have communicated more effectively the scope of the transformation. Fighting a global recession that impacted the company more than most was bad enough, but trying to transform the enterprise at the same time caused some disquiet within the organization. Luckily, during our journey we did stop some of the initiatives, and we improved on our communications.

When you embark on any kind of substantive transformation change, you need to ensure that you implement appropriate processes and controls to increase the chance of success. Most importantly, do not underestimate the importance of communication. Total clarity is required so that all key stakeholders are absolutely aligned, including the senior management team and the board. Doing this requires a comprehensive communication strategy and plan with an abundance of dialogue and regular updates built in. Assign a senior person to manage the project and include appropriate metrics to ensure that the project is delivered on time and within budget.

12. Create an Effective Communication Plan

The importance of an effective communication plan, especially during a major transformation or when you are dealing with significant global shocks, cannot be overstated. I know this from difficult experience as CEO of Harsco when we implemented our major transformation strategy at the same time the 2008 global economic crisis began. But even without the global economic meltdown, the lesson is the same. The leader of the organization must personally champion the communication plan and work to ensure that the plan is comprehensive and targets all stakeholders, including the board of directors, shareholders, sell-side analysts, and the senior management team. Here are a couple of lessons I learned from my experience:

> » *Work with an outside professional communication and public-relations team.* In Harsco's case, an outside public relations team could have helped us communicate more effectively about the tremendous headwinds and challenges the company faced and what we intended to do about them. At the same time, an outside team could have helped us present a unified message to both internal and external constituents about the transformational journey we had embarked on and the impact of the global economic shocks.

> » *An effective and focused communication plan is a lifeline.* A well-crafted communication plan needs to be a top priority item for the CEO, and it can be a true lifeline as well. A professionally managed communication plan is not only indispensable, but it can sometimes be the difference between success and failure.

13. Effectively Define, Manage, and Communicate Transformational Change

The OneHarsco optimization initiative was one of the strategies that underpinned our transformational journey that began in 2008. The initiative sought to materially reduce our cost structure by improving overall operational efficiency and effectiveness while bringing the company together culturally. There were three major objectives with this strategy:

> » *Materially reduce the fixed-cost structure* (due to highly disaggregated business footprint) and thereby lower the overall break-even point of the company. This would be accomplished by fully integrating locations and by eliminating some regional and country administrative centers, as well as reducing the level of fixed assets employed in the business.

> » *Develop new exceptional capabilities*, such as a globally integrated supply chain, a global shared-services center, and a Lean continuous-improvement discipline. The objective of these new capabilities was to capture scale benefits of operating globally across multiple platforms and be more innovative. Another objective was to connect each business segment so that there would be more cross-selling, as well as assistance in penetrating key countries where Harsco already had a presence.

> » *Rebrand the company and create a unified company culture.* As part of this effort, we envisioned bringing the executives together in one location (Harrisburg) in order to foster collaboration and teamwork.

The OneHarsco initiative was also intended to align the businesses into four operating segments. Each segment would retain its entrepreneurial culture while at the same time significantly improve efficiencies and increase capabilities. This meant that the four segments would be responsible for all operating decisions relating to the customer and included sales and marketing, research and development, site operations, customer support and service, and all other related operational activities. Global functions like finance, legal, risk management, human resources, and information technology would be the responsibility of the corporate office operating under a matrix system.

While there were many lessons I learned from spearheading this initiative, here are three of the key ones:

> » *Clearly define the scope of outside consultants and do not deviate.* Since this project was so important, with such a significant potential for cost reductions, we hired an outside consulting firm to assist us, which is normal practice. The consultants did what many consultants do—they naturally expanded the scope. Regrettably, we allowed the scope of the project to increase as it went along because of the substantial business case the consultants made for potential further cost savings. Although we finally did put the consultants back on the original path, we lost some valuable time.

> » *Stick to your business model.* As explained in detail in chapter 4, "Business Model," choosing the right business model is vitally important. In our case, the potential rewards of becoming a fully integrated enterprise, as proposed by the consultants, were difficult to ignore because the estimated savings were substantial. What we discovered, after due diligence, is that it was extremely expensive and time-consuming to achieve an integrated-enterprise model. In hindsight, it is clear that we would have had better results had we stayed with my original concept of the hybrid or matrix model that we ultimately called OneHarsco. In our defense, it was hard to ignore the potential cost savings of an integrated enterprise, since the decisions were made in the middle of a deep global recession and we were dealing with tumbling sales. While we did reverse course and return to our original vision of a hybrid (matrix) model, we lost some valuable time in the realization of our transformational strategy.

> » *The OneHarsco optimization initiative worked.* The overall fixed-cost structure of the company was significantly reduced. The

company also realized savings from our integrated sourcing and supply-chain initiative beginning in late 2011. The India shared-services center started paying dividends almost immediately in its first full year of operation in 2011. Two of the four segments that embraced the Lean continuous-improvement discipline with vigor made a meaningful positive impact and improved their results staring in 2010. The rebranding and connecting of all the segments of the company also benefited Harsco in many ways, including cross-selling of services and products, better cooperation in developing emerging markets, and establishment of a foundation for building a more unified culture.

14. Think Differently and Adapt to Change

My favorite example of thinking differently or out-of-the box was captured brilliantly by Rich Cohen in a 2012 *Wall Street Journal* article on lessons learned from the great businessman Samuel Zemurray, the so-called Banana Man. The takeaway message from the Zemurray story is that a simple problem requires a simple solution. Here is the story:

> In the late 1920s, United Fruit and Sam's company were trying to acquire the same piece of land, a fertile expanse that straddled the border of Honduras and Guatemala. But the land seemed to have two rightful owners, one in Honduras, the other in Guatemala. While U. F. hired lawyers and commissioned studies, trying to determine the legal property holder, Zemurray simply purchased the land twice, once from each owner.[59]

Dr. Ian Bremmer, in *Every Nation for Itself*, plainly states the importance of adaptability and original thinking: "Among multinational companies, it's the adapters that will be most successful—those that understand the changing competitive landscape and are agile enough to exploit the advantages it provides."[60]

One of the early challenges I encountered in my tenure as a CEO was getting some of the global leadership participants to think more out-of-the box. Although we made substantive progress in acting proactively, I still had to push hard to move some key initiatives forward. My experience is that when it takes the encouragement of the CEO to get something done, usually the cause is cultural. Let me provide two examples:

» *Emerging markets.* The culture was such that expanding in the emerging markets was not always a high-priority matter. Some in the organization were content with being primarily a European company. The organization had no presence in India and was on the verge of becoming a nonfactor in China. With substantial input and involvement from me, through a globalization strategic initiative, in just four years we successfully increased our revenues in the emerging economies by 50 percent. We had success throughout the world, particularly in China, India, and Latin America.

» *Joint ventures and strategic alliances.* I believed that future success for growing organically and accelerating our innovation initiatives (and learning) was through joint ventures and strategic alliances. Just like the emerging-markets strategy, I encountered some cultural resistance. Again, with substantial input and involvement from me, we successfully signed some vital joint ventures and strategic alliances, particularly in emerging markets. Some of Harsco's best contract wins in 2011 and 2012 (as well as some in early 2013) resulted from the well-structured joint ventures that we put in place as part of the strategy we developed in early 2008. In addition, in 2011 we signed a record number of strategic alliances throughout the world that were centered on innovation. We were building future lifelines.

15. Carefully Consider Investments in High-Capital Expenditure Businesses

As a general principle, any business that has a heavy burden of capital expenditures should be anathema to leaders unless there is a predictable and sustainable revenue stream. It's usually best to operate a business that is capital-expenditures light. Businesses with heavy capital expenditures will likely raise the return risks, especially in highly cyclical markets. This is another lesson I learned from my Harsco experience, because two of Harsco's largest businesses required heavy capital expenditures and operated in cyclical markets.

However, as a CEO, you should know that an effective antidote to this burden and elevated risk is to put in place a highly rigorous and disciplined capital-allocation process so that every dollar is invested efficiently and implementing an innovative business model. (See chapter 6, "Exceptional Capabilities," and chapter 4, "Business Model.") Moreover, you need to ensure that the business has a predictable and sustainable cash-flow stream with a cash return that is in excess of its cost of capital. With these elements in place and with flawless execution, it is possible to minimize your company's risk to heavy capital expenditures and actually prosper. The large US oil companies are good examples of enterprises that successfully invest large sums on capital projects.

16. Invest and Grow "Niche" Businesses

Leaders and boards of directors leading highly diversified companies need to answer this question: Is it a better recipe to build an enterprise for the long-term around high-margin, high-return niche businesses that require minimal capital expenditures and generate substantial free cash flow, or is it better to continue with the more traditional path of balancing a mix of businesses in the portfolio? It is important to note that choosing solely the niche business strategy will most likely require the courage to divest some core businesses.

We had considerable success in first identifying and then rebranding the niche businesses within Harsco—Harsco Rail, Harsco Industrial, and Harsco Minerals—and then successfully globalizing them in a short period of about four years. In hindsight, our lesson learned here was that it would have perhaps been better to invest more in these businesses so that they could have grown faster, while at the same time investing less in the larger capital-intensive businesses.

17. Evaluate the Business Portfolio Early in Your Tenure

Newly appointed leaders are usually given a grace period to take bold strategic actions, and it's time you should exploit if possible. Once this window of opportunity is closed, a leader may have to use considerable internal political capital to effect a similar change. These actions typically include selling or acquiring a business, making leadership changes within the management team, or taking the company in a different direction.

In my discussion with various leaders as well as my own experience over the years, an effective approach is to retain a high-quality management consulting firm to review the portfolio. The strategic review of the portfolio should focus on several key areas, including fit of each business; regional and global trends; end-market conditions and the long-term viability of those markets; competitive landscape; customers and the dynamics of the customer base; cost structure; and capabilities of the company.

The results of this engagement can be used by the leader to commence a vigorous dialogue with the board and the senior management team, which can be the foundation for developing a strategic road map and long-term vision for the company.

18. Be Audacious When Undertaking a Major Restructuring Action

A common trap that leaders fall into if their organization requires restructuring is lack of bold action. My observation is that anything less risks a cure that is worse than the condition. Such timid approaches usually force the enterprise to take a series of restructuring actions as they try to feel their way through the fog of turbulence and uncertain markets. Not only does this approach bring possible risks, but it ultimately may harm the reputation of the organization, the leader, and the board of directors. The cure to this potential illness is an audacious plan. Over the years, I observed that organizations that announce a comprehensive and bold restructuring plan are usually rewarded by investors. Conversely, enterprises that announce multiple plans that span several years are usually punished.

A more audacious plan can possibly save both reputations and money, and it minimizes the time an organization is distracted and not moving forward. An aggressive and audacious restructuring plan should include the following elements:

» *Scope.* Leaders need to think big! It is imperative not to undersize or underestimate what it will take to right the organization. Your precocious characteristics will be of great use in these situations.

» *One-time event.* As noted above, absolutely no repeat or multiple restructuring actions. Develop your bold, audacious plan, take action to implement it, and lead your organization forward.

» *Public-relations plan.* Make sure that your shareholders, employees, and analysts have a clear understanding of the scope, timing, cost, and benefits of the plan. In the scheme of things, this communication plan is just as important as the actual restructuring action. Use an outside public-relations firm to assist with this important communication plan.

» *Executive accountability.* Assign this project to your best executive. The future success and credibility of the company is at stake, so don't delegate this to a junior person or someone other than your best.

» *Outside assistance.* Use an outside top-tier consulting firm to assist with the scope of your plan and, if appropriate, its execution. As discussed earlier in lesson learned 13, however, consultants need to be carefully managed.

19. Rebuild Your Balance Sheet

The twin global shocks of the US financial crisis and the European sovereign debt crisis have damaged the balance sheet of many companies, particularly enterprises carrying an elevated level of debt before the great recession. As a former CFO, I have a particular interest and affinity for managing a balance sheet and what actions are most appropriate for doing that effectively. A strong balance sheet is extremely important to company growth and strong management. Here are some levers that a leader can pull to restore a company's balance sheet:

- » *Sell underperforming and nonperforming assets.* Take the opportunity to divest assets that are idle or not earning their cost of capital. Compile an inventory of all assets including land, buildings, product lines, and other potentially valuable assets like patents. Assign an executive to oversee this very important strategic project.

- » *Reevaluate the portfolio with a long-term view.* A reexamination of the portfolio is a key responsibility of the CEO. Often this results in the divestiture of parts of the business that no longer fit the vision of the enterprise. Get outside assistance on this and, of course, involve the board.

- » *Conserve cash.* Reduce costs and capital expenditures to conserve cash.

- » *Restructure pension plans.* Freeze all defined-benefit pension plans and convert to defined-contribution plans. Make sure that the pension assets are being well managed.

- » *Generate cash from other sources.* Examine opportunities to generate cash and income from royalty and licensing fees.

- » *Raise capital.* Capital can be raised through an equity offering. There are multiple paths that can be taken. Work with the board and your investment bankers.

20. Unleashing the Power of Scalability

Leaders must understand the two models of scalability. One model requires a relatively large investment (e.g., Starbucks or McDonald's), and the other model requires a much more limited amount of investment (e.g., a software provider, such as Microsoft).

The first category of scalability requires investment in leases or stores, equipment, people, and inventory, and the process is relatively slow. However, due to the highly replicable model and efficiencies gained from sourcing, branding and marketing, process improvements, and limited corporate staff growth, these organizations make formidable competitors. On the other hand, under the second category, a majority of the revenue dollars quickly go straight to the bottom line because the cost of scalability is minimal. In either case, a relatively significant portion of every incremental dollar of revenue should flow to the bottom line if a business is properly scaled. Enterprises that can skillfully scale their business model have the opportunity to create considerable value.

All those incremental revenue dollars that flow to the bottom line can have a significant impact on all the key metrics, including return on invested capital, gross margins, and operating margins. Scalability can provide a considerable competitive advantage to a company, and it needs to be part of the generative thinking process in developing the business model.

My favorite example of the power of scalability, however, can be found in education. With the explosion of technology, the ability to scale education has been totally transformed. The traditional method, with its high fixed costs along with a limited ability to reach a large pool of students, is under attack because of technology. This is because the power of scalability here is unmatched. Let me provide an example that can be found in the book *College (Un)bound* by Jeffrey J. Selingo. Most people today have heard of the Khan Academy, which is a free online tutoring website with thousands of short educational videos. Selingo tells the story of when Kahn started back in 2009 with hundreds of students viewing the videos in a given month. He goes on to write that "just three years later, Khan Academy lessons are viewed by more than four million people a month."[61]

Lessons Learned: Uncertainty and Turbulence

21. Deal Decisively with Global Shocks and Economic Turbulence

As I have mentioned, there is a lot that we can learn from mountaineering. In their book *Extreme Alpinism: Climbing Light, Fast, and High*, Mark F. Twight and James Martin capture the essence of how business leaders need to think and act during extreme economic conditions:

Nobody controls a situation in the mountains. It is vanity to imagine one can. Instead, grow comfortable with giving up control and acting within chaos and uncertainty. Attempting to dominate constantly changing circumstances in the mountains or to fight the loss of control serves only to increase fear and multiply its effects. Embrace the inherent lack of control and focus on applying skills and ideals to the situation.[62]

Professor Richard A. D'Aveni gives this advice about weathering massive economic storms well in his book *Beating the Commodity Trap*: "A sharp economic downturn causes the perfect storm. Market prices and benefits deteriorate as customers seek bargains—and demand simply evaporates. Countermeasures are necessary to survive. Batten down the hatches to weather the storm. Goal is to maximize cash flow."[63]

Harsco traveled through the most turbulent and difficult time in its modern history while I was CEO, and I learned many lessons about leadership from the experience. The first was to avoid panic, and the second was to be proactive. The third was to confront the facts squarely and prepare for the worst outcome while hoping for the best. The fourth important lesson was to act fast; in a period of high turbulence, speed is paramount. Speed is particularly important relative to the fifth lesson, the need to significantly lower your cost structure and the break-even point. The sixth is to conserve as much cash as possible. Leaders in these crisis situations must be fanatical about building cash reserves to weather the storm so that their organizations emerge from the difficult times stronger and ready to perform.

Other key lifeline lessons include reducing capital expenditures; communicating frequently with all your organization's stakeholders; retaining all of your key customers; maintaining a strong balance sheet; and reevaluating the effectiveness of all those on your team. There are several other key factors to consider, such as rethinking your business model. It is essential that your business model is agile and built on variable costs as opposed to fixed costs. Also, seize opportunities as they become available to take market share from competitors and to purchase strategic assets at a discount.

The most important lesson learned from recent major global shocks is that companies that are well prepared will usually outperform the less prepared. Visionary leaders who clearly understand that the preparation for difficult economic times needs to occur during good times will be virtually immunized from the illness that can strike the less prepared. It is imperative that an ample supply of lifelines be built over a long horizon (decades) to prepare for any unforeseen yet inevitable global shocks.

22. Analyze Possible Scenarios and Prepare for the Worst

Mountaineering rule number one states, "Hope for the best but plan for the worst." When I was Harsco CEO, although like many other companies we routinely performed scenario analysis, no one predicted the precipitous drops in the construction-services orders and pricing that occurred as the result of two extreme global shocks. We also underestimated the overall deceleration of the European and North American nonresidential construction markets. There was no historical precedent for what was happening in our end-markets, so we found ourselves not adequately prepared to deal with mountaineering rule number two, "Getting up the mountain is optional, getting down the mountain is mandatory."

We ultimately made it down the mountain with difficulties, but not without lessons learned. These lessons include the wisdom of hiring an in-house economist, putting together a more diverse team to come up with extreme worst-case scenarios (perhaps even outside market experts to help us think through these scenarios), and using robust economic models to assist in the development of the scenarios. Still, given the severity of the collapse of the construction markets and the long recovery period, even that action might not have predicted the worst-case scenario. This point was made by Bob Tita in a 2013 *Wall Street Journal* article that stated, "Five years after commercial construction market's collapse, utilization rates and sales remain soft."[64]

Lessons Learned: Execution and Focus

23. Integrate Acquisitions Immediately

It is essential to fully integrate acquisitions into the acquiring company's structure and culture. It sounds like obvious advice, but many companies allow acquired companies to operate independently and thus encounter problems like

- » diminished effectiveness of the acquiring company's culture,
- » loss of potential cost synergies, and
- » derailed or hampered corporate strategy alignment.

One caveat—and as outlined under the decentralized model in chapter 4, "Business Model"—it may not be necessary to completely follow this rule if the parent company has a strong entrepreneurial culture, is a consistently high performer, does not have the majority of its business units exposed to highly cyclical end-markets, and has key enterprise controls in place. Nonetheless, key exceptional capabilities, such as innovation and integrated supply chain, should be harnessed irrespective of the business model.

My advice for leaders is to ensure that you have a comprehensive integration plan that maximizes all potential benefits and is carefully designed to fit the business model, exceptional capabilities, and the culture of the enterprise. A top senior-level executive should be appointed to develop and oversee the plan. The integration plan needs to be part of the acquisition playbook, and it must be developed early in the process, long before the transaction is consummated.

24. Do Not Focus Primarily on the Competition

The myth that successful companies focus primarily on beating the competition is simply not true. Visionary companies focus primarily on improving their own performance and leave the competition mostly to its own devices.

A management team obsessed with the competition loses sight of the more essential focus on continuous improvement, innovation, and delivering a superior service or product to the customer. As one of today's premier college football coaches, Nick Saban, says about competition, it is much better "for people not to worry about the opposition … and know if they do their job correctly they're going to be successful." Thinking any other way, Saban says, just allows the competition "to determine the outcome."[65]

25. Do Not Rely on a Single Metric

In 2002, Harsco adopted Economic Value Added (EVA), which was developed by the firm Stern Stewart in New York City. EVA was chosen as the key metric for making capital expenditure (organic growth investment) decisions, and it was also used for the short-term (annual) incentive plan. Later, we added EVA for our long-term incentive plan. EVA is measured by taking net operating profit after-tax (NOPAT) and subtracting from it a capital charge. The capital charge is determined by multiplying the total invested capital in the business by the cost of capital.

EVA provides a measure of true economic profit, taking into account not only traditional accounting-based profit measures but also a charge for the use of the total capital (debt and equity) employed to create those profits. EVA works on the principle that capital is not free and that investors expect to be rewarded on the capital. Accordingly, the fundamental litmus test behind any capital investment decision is whether or not it will create more value than an alternative investment opportunity with similar risk. Capital is a limited resource, and it must be managed prudently. Thus, capital allocation is critical to the long-term success of an enterprise.

EVA is a powerful metric, and I'm a believer. On the incentive side, EVA promotes a culture of performance and ownership. It links incentives to value creation. It provides accountability for invested capital and a way to reward management for a positive change in EVA compared with the previous year.

We created a one-page "EVA Drivers" document so that everyone could visually see all the major levers that could be pulled to create value.

However, we made it clear to everyone in the organization that EVA was not a panacea or a silver bullet, and it wasn't a replacement for leadership, good judgment, and execution of strategy. Still, even as good as it was, the use of a single metric, even EVA, has its downside. Here's a brief overview of these pitfalls:

» EVA is a good tool for evaluating investments, but just like any model the devil is in the details. EVA, like the discounted cash-flow models, relies on assumptions to determine if value is destroyed or created. One needs to get the assumptions right, particularly in a highly capital-intensive business where the time horizon for investments are usually long. The dialogue over assumptions needs to be vigorous within the organization because it makes the difference between creating sustainable value and destroying value. All time-honored assumptions about the business must be challenged. The business model and market volatility are also important variables in this equation. All of these factors need to be properly weighed when developing the EVA assumptions. Otherwise, the actual results could look dramatically different from the projected numbers.

» EVA, in the short-term, can benefit overinvestment because NOPAT will usually exceed the capital charge during any economic boom period. The problem occurs when the lines cross—that is, when the capital charge exceeds NOPAT. This can happen if a company gets caught with a lot of capital during a severe economic storm and NOPAT drops precipitously due to pricing pressures and fewer orders. It's very important to recognize this potential pitfall and, more importantly, to avoid it.

» EVA is good for the annual incentive payout but is not ideal for a long-term plan. With the annual incentive plan, considerable care needs to be taken in setting the EVA improvement target for the year. EVA works better if the management team is together over a long horizon because timing can benefit or hurt sometimes in potentially unfair ways. Suffice it to say that EVA is too complex to be used for a long-term incentive determinate and that different metrics should be considered, including total shareholder return, free cash flow, and cash return on invested capital. There are numerous variations of these three prominent metrics for measuring long-term value creation. Choose the one that best fits the culture of the company because they are all equally effective.

Lessons Learned: Board-Related Matters

26. Don't Make Too Many Board Changes

Your relationship with the board of directors is tremendously important because your fate ultimately rests in their hands. I learned this lesson by advocating for changing the profile of our board in response to the retirement of several directors. As the incoming chairman and CEO, I believed at the time that the board was underrepresented with operating executives and particularly with sitting or recently retired CEOs. So in the course of approximately two years, the board profile changed considerably with the addition of a number of operating executives who were recruited mostly from large companies. These new directors joined the company during a period of unprecedented change, mainly the transformation initiative and the great recession.

With perfect hindsight, I see that perhaps we should have implemented the board succession plan over a period of at least five years or possibly longer instead of about two. Moreover, we should have recognized the benefit of retaining several excellent directors by simply advocating for a rule change that would have allowed them to serve past their seventieth birthday. This would have allowed for a longer transition period to build the board, it would have retained key historical perspective, and it would have avoided the need to immediately recruit new outside directors. Having this institutional knowledge, particularly during a period of unprecedented change and economic tumult, would have been valuable.

The lesson learned is to avoid rushing a decision to make board changes, since it carries with it potential risk. Board changes should be made over a long horizon so the potential risk to board culture and the loss of historical perspective are all minimized.

27. Use an Effective Internal Sourcing Process to Recruit Board Members

A highly potent succession-planning process for the board of directors is essential to establish. The CEO and chairman, along with the lead director and the chairman of the governance and nominating committee, must map a long-term vision spanning at least ten years so that new board members can be blended effectively.

Some boards rely solely on professional board search firms for their pool of candidates, others rely on recommendations from existing board members, and some use a blend of the two. My personal experience is that relying solely on a search firm is not always effective. Most search firms have a limited pool of highly qualified directors, so you may be relying on luck to secure the right candidate. In addition, a search firm is not a disinterested party, since it stands to gain by your acceptance of its candidate. By solely following the search-firm process, I believe a company risks losing out on better candidates. I believe boards should use the blend of both internal and external resources to recruit members, with a strong bias toward the internal sourcing process.

The governance and nominating committee, along with the board of directors, should design an effective internal sourcing system that considers factors like culture, diversity, skill, perspective, and the critical precocious characteristics outlined in this book. Furthermore, this group needs to ensure that there is a perfect blend of backgrounds on the board. The required skills of independent board members need to be carefully analyzed and dialogued, and they should include such areas as operations, engineering, innovation, finance, global experience, and people with digital backgrounds. Diversity should include a healthy number of females and minorities. A highly diverse board will most likely enhance the culture and the performance of the board, and ultimately that of the company they serve.

28. Create a Solid CEO Succession-Planning Process

My personal belief is that the CEO should come from inside the company. If that doesn't happen, then the board of directors—whose most important job is CEO continuity—has fallen short of adequately delivering on one its key roles. That's why the board must ensure that there is an adequate pipeline of candidates (preferably internal to the organization) so that the succession process can begin within a reasonable timeframe. The CEO succession planning process needs to be robust, and it needs to be regularly dialogued by the board.

If the board perceives, for whatever reason, that a CEO change is necessary for nonperformance, then a mutual consent approach is a win-win scenario for both the board and the CEO. This approach should cause minimal internal and external disruption. However, the process should be managed carefully, because an unplanned exit by a CEO may raise a red flag. This can possibly be avoided by simply following a common-sense approach, and experienced and seasoned boards should have little trouble negotiating these familiar public-relations waters both inside and outside the organization. The *Wall Street Journal* has been full of examples, particularly in the last few years, of unplanned CEO exits that were well managed by boards. These cases should be studied by leaders and board members with the objective of learning.

29. Decide Whether to Combine or Separate the Roles of Chairman and CEO

I have experience and perspective on the matter of combining or separating the roles of the chairman and CEO. Just like many complex issues in business, no simple answer is possible. You can't arrive at the right answer without exercising sound judgment informed by a deep knowledge of the facts particular to the enterprise and a keen understanding of the composition of the board.

Combining the roles of the chairman and CEO provides an efficient, effective, and desirable leadership model, but following this path requires a framework of strict accountability and responsibility and a strong, independent lead director. Using this model requires that the majority of the board members are independent within the meaning of the NYSE listing standards and that members follow modern best-practices on corporate governance. All this information concerning guidelines is easy to access in proxy statements and company websites. However, for this model to be effective, a true and well-respected leader with extensive leadership experience and perspective should be appointed as the lead director. Boards should avoid appointments that are perfunctory in nature.

One of the most important reasons for combining the two roles is the benefit of a unified leadership. The individual who holds both titles, however, needs to ensure that a perfect balance is struck between the two roles. It helps if the individual has extensive experience in both roles in order to be highly effective. In addition, there are certain cultures like the Chinese where the chairman's position is revered, and thus it is helpful to the CEO if he has both titles. I experienced this firsthand in China and several other countries as well.

Separating the chairman and CEO roles requires considerable dialogue at the board level to avoid serious conflicts. The most obvious conflict is between the CEO and the chairman, which could slow decision making down considerably. There are scenarios, however, where separating the two roles makes sense. One example is when a new CEO is appointed with no prior board or CEO leadership experience. If the composition of the board is strong and filled with a least one retired chairman and CEO, it may make sense to separate the two roles. Later, if circumstances warrant a change, the positions can be combined.

30. Join at Least One Board

I believe that a leader must find the time to serve on at least one company board, either private or public. I made the mistake of not joining a board during my tenure as CEO even though I had numerous opportunities to do so, and I regret this decision. This is an area in which the board of directors can be helpful by insisting that the CEO serve on another company's board.

From my viewpoint, there are two highly important reasons for the CEO to join a board as an independent director. First, it is a critical lifeline for the CEO. Not only will the CEO be exposed to how other organizations operate, which is invaluable, it is also an opportunity for the CEO to be exposed to other successful leaders (board members).

Secondly, if the CEO's tenure is unexpectedly cut short, this board seat is highly important to use as a foundation for obtaining additional board positions. Just as it is easier to find employment while employed, the same principle applies to board seats.

Takeaways

All leaders make mistakes. What is important as a leader is to minimize the number of errors in judgment. The most salient lessons learned during my tenure as a leader include the following:

» Always rely on your instincts or intuition.

» Do not assume anything or take anything for granted.

» Do not try to do too much too fast; it could cause problems.

» Use the right metric or metrics in making investment decisions and incentive payments.

» Choose a world-class human-resources chief as your most trusted advisor. Establish appropriate mechanisms to embed and assess people characteristics. Promote from within, particularly at the senior management level.

» Remember, your job as CEO is not to make friends but to get results.

» Invest in niche businesses that provide a sustained competitive advantage.

» Carry a healthy level of skepticism.

» Treat everyone equally and with respect.

» Ensure that board actions are the result of good judgment, perspective, and wisdom.

» Manage change well. An effective communication plan is a true lifeline.

» Organizations must have the ability to think differently and adapt to change.

» Evaluate business portfolio early in tenure. Strategic restructuring actions require audacious thinking.

» Integrate acquisitions immediately.

» Allow for a period of inner reflection and growth. Be proactive in protecting your reputation and position.

» Maintain a strong balance sheet and create a winning culture. Decisive action is required to counter global shocks and economic turbulence.

» Effectively use the power of scalability.

CHAPTER 6

Exceptional Capabilities

We are what we repeatedly do.
Excellence, then, is not an act, but a habit.
—Aristotle[66]

In order to successfully and safely ascend their most challenging summit, elite mountaineers rely on their exceptional skills and technical knowledge. Enterprises must also possess what I call *exceptional capabilities* if they are to successfully climb their ultimate summit—that is, the creation of an elite and sustainable enterprise. An important step in creating such an enterprise is following the twenty exceptional capabilities detailed in this chapter. These exceptional capabilities represent another set of fundamental leader and enterprise lifelines that are essential to the long-term health and success of an enterprise.

Leaders willing to apply these proven practices should see improved performance and value-creation potential, while achieving a competitive advantage that could differentiate a company in the global marketplace. These exceptional capabilities can be particularly powerful and value-creating if they are deployed by an enterprise that is built on these characteristics:

- » adaptable and proactive
- » global in reach and mind-set
- » driven by an innovative and entrepreneurial business model
- » generates prodigious free cash flow and strong operating results
- » founded on a clear mission statement and strong core values
- » home to an exceptional management team

Build Your Lifelines with Exceptional Capabilities

The twenty exceptional capabilities that I unveil in this chapter are validated by almost four decades of leadership practice and by keen observation and study. They are in no particular order of importance, since it's impossible to know which capability should be top priority for an enterprise's unique set of circumstances. Here is the list:

1. Enhance the cash-conversion cycle.
2. Improve capital efficiency.
3. Use an integrated global supply chain.
4. Set up global shared services.
5. Employ Lean and Six-Sigma.
6. Execute a product-management strategy.
7. Take advantage of pricing power and value selling.
8. Implement a variable cost model.
9. Review the global legal and tax structure.
10. Develop exceptional project-management skills.
11. Focus on brand development.
12. Invest in science and innovation.
13. Design an effective talent-management system.
14. Monitor sales cadence, backlog, and forecasting.
15. Do a real-time scan of the environment.

16. View information technology as a strategic asset.

17. Seek out joint ventures and strategic alliances.

18. Target strategic acquisitions.

19. Maintain disciplined growth.

20. Identify frontier markets.

Some of the capabilities discussed below are expanded upon in other sections of this book, but the twenty exceptional capabilities listed here can be further classified into one of three essential philosophical strategies: *optimization, innovation,* and *globalization.* Enterprises that focus on these three areas, along with the other essential lifelines outlined in the book, should bring success through sustained high performance.

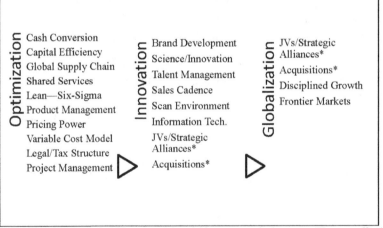

*Joint Ventures/Strategic Alliances and Acquisitions serve a dual purpose. They are effective vehicles for growth, and they are also a powerful mechanism for innovation (as well as learning).

Optimization

Optimization includes exceptional capabilities or skills that deliver the products and services of the organization at the lowest cost possible, realize the highest prices possible, and provide the enterprise with a distinctive advantage. Optimization includes the first ten exceptional capabilities.

1. Enhance the Cash-Conversion Cycle

The cash-conversion cycle measures the speed of cash and working-capital efficiency. The formula is: accounts receivable days + inventory days – accounts payable days = cash conversion cycle.

Some businesses put a significant effort into receiving advance payments from customers—an excellent practice to follow, if possible. For example, on large, specialized production orders, some manufacturers insist on advance payments as well as progress payments. Another innovative idea is used in the retail business with the practice of gift cards and loading dollars on store cards. However, if advance payments are received, you will have to modify the calculation to include these advances. In these cases, the enterprise would have to deduct (–) the advance payment days and accounts payable days (–) from accounts receivable and inventory days to determine (=) the cash-conversion-cycle number. The objective, of course, is to arrive at the lowest number possible, with the best-case scenario being a negative number.

When Dell first developed its innovative online ordering business, the computer giant was posting a negative cash-conversion-cycle number—that is, Dell's customers were funding working capital for the company. While this scenario is bliss, for most enterprises it's impractical to expect to achieve a negative cash-conversion number. Nonetheless, the CEO should not accept the working-capital status quo and should set improvement targets that are monitored closely. Many of the capabilities outlined in this chapter, such as Lean and Six-Sigma, help improve working capital efficiency, which in turn generates incremental cash. Since cash is essential to the health of an enterprise, the cash-conversion cycle is a lifeline that can't be ignored.

2. Improve Capital Efficiency

Capital efficiency is all about improving the return on invested capital from capital expenditures. The key variables that play into this include what you pay for the asset, maintenance costs, engineering design, and the EVA generated by the asset employed. A key metric for capital efficiency is the EVA generated by the investment divided by the total cost of ownership of that asset. The higher the number, the more value is being created.

There are a lot of levers to pull to improve capital efficiency. For example, you can

> » create EVA through improving pricing and contract terms;
>
> » reduce the cost of the asset by global sourcing and procurement practices and thus the total cost of ownership;
>
> » improve maintenance and reduce costs through Lean and Six-Sigma and by adopting global best practices;
>
> » redesign and reengineer a process that results in less equipment or the use of a different type of equipment that is less expensive;
>
> » adhere to a global standard for all equipment to improve efficiencies;
>
> » use embedded technology in the equipment to provide real-time performance data that will ultimately lower costs;
>
> » enter into cross-rental agreements with customers and competitors (in certain industries); or
>
> » innovate to transform the delivery of the product or service.

For businesses that require heavy capital expenditures to sustain and grow the enterprise, this is an area of opportunity. A focused effort on capital expenditures saves considerable cash that can be redeployed elsewhere or returned to shareholders through dividends and share repurchases.

3. Use an Integrated Global Supply Chain

A modern multinational company cannot survive without a high-quality sourcing group; talented, empowered people to run it; and potent global supply-chain software to manage the function. It is essential that this group reports to the CEO—if possible, locate your chief procurement officer near the source of the majority of your goods and services. An effective global supply-chain group can create formidable economic value for an enterprise through the development of strategic relationships with suppliers.

Apple is one of the best examples of how a company can use a global supply chain to drive input costs down, find the best partners, and deliver a superior product. In the book *Inside Apple*, author Adam Lashinsky provides some revealing insights into how Apple manages and benefits from its supply chains. "Apple doesn't own the saw, and it doesn't own the company that owns the saw," Lashinsky writes. "It also doesn't staff the factory where the saw will be used. But it absolutely has an opinion as to which saw its supplier will use. It's a new form of vertical integration; where once a manufacturer would own every step of the process, Apple now controls each step without owning any of it."[67] Another advantage of this structure is that costs now become variable as opposed to fixed.

4. Set Up Global Shared Services

A global shared-services center is a must capability for a modern multinational firm. Currently, India and cities like Hyderabad are the ideal place for these services, particularly if your company needs services in the heavy-engineering and information-technology sector. Not only will the move lower the overall cost of doing business, but overall capability will likely improve due to the high-quality labor pool in India.

Another current shared-services hot spot is San Jose, Costa Rica, due to its high English-centric literacy rate and business-friendly atmosphere. Note that it's desirable to maintain two centers to avoid disruptions in business due to instability and other unforeseen changes in a key resource country. The global shared-services center should report to the corporate CIO, CFO, or an executive vice president responsible for enterprise services.

5. Employ Lean and Six-Sigma

Organizations need to have a culture that believes in and promotes continuous improvement to achieve the status of a high-performance enterprise. That's why I believe that Lean or Six-Sigma should be one of the core values of an organization.

Six-Sigma is a continuous-improvement discipline focused on reducing process variability. It refers to 3.4 defects per one million opportunities, a level that is considered to represent world-class quality performance. Six-Sigma was originally developed by Motorola in the 1980s. Just like Lean, it is an effective mechanism for the CEO to use in changing and shaping the culture of the enterprise. As I mentioned earlier, I was fortunate to attend a Motorola Six-Sigma class on improving the quality of the finance function in the early 1990s. Harsco used this tool very effectively to transform the global financial reporting process of the company.

While Six-Sigma's focus is on identifying and removing the root cause of defects, the focus of Lean is on eliminating waste. Lean traces its roots to the Japanese automobile industry in the 1980s and mainly the Toyota production system. Unlike traditional cost-reduction initiatives, Lean is a powerful tool that is not about doing more with less but doing more with existing resources. Eliminating waste and inefficiency frees up critical resources needed to scale the business without increasing overhead costs.

The method of execution that underpins Lean is called the Kaizen Breakthrough Event. The vital process to execute the Lean discipline is rooted in the Japanese term *Kaizen*, which means "change for the good." Kaizen events take place over five highly focused days between extensive prework preparation and post-Kaizen sustainment. Kaizen events enable people from all parts and levels of the organization to participate.

Most Kaizen recommendations are implemented immediately. Lean is a formidable tool that can be used in any part or function of the organization. It can be used with equal effectiveness in manufacturing companies, service organizations, and business processes.

6. Execute a Product-Management Strategy

A sound product-management strategy consolidates the power and responsibility for the product life cycle under one person as opposed to fragmenting it across multiple functions. Giving a product manager decision-making responsibility and accountability for pricing, innovation, design, and other critical elements of a product life cycle usually culminates in a positive transformational change that gets results. Note that this product manager must be an A-player with strong leadership characteristics (particularly proactive), a deep product knowledge, and an ability to work across functions. It is a good idea to benchmark this practice with other companies before you embark on this potentially transformative change. Finally, it's also recommended that outside experts be utilized in its implementation.

We implemented a product-management strategy in one of our key businesses with strong results. There are a multitude of companies that employ this strategy successfully, and they can be contacted through various channels including the elite consulting practices that have specialization in this area and board members with this type of experience. One of the best examples of a company that is organized and structured around its products, I have discovered through my research, is Google. Google is organized into seven product-focused business groups. Each executive of a product group has full responsibility and accountability for results.

7. Take Advantage of Pricing Power and Value Selling

Pricing power is the nirvana of business. Companies with pricing leverage have the ability to invest in building an elite enterprise through high investment in innovation, hiring the best, most talented people. The end result is that these companies are highly efficient and scalable. Apple and its desirable operating margins is one shining example of this strategy.

Unfortunately, not all companies have this pricing power because of competition with other companies selling essentially the same product or service, a problem that is exacerbated during a major economic downturn. Still, many of the capabilities outlined in this chapter can help a company to overcome pricing obstacles, particularly value selling.

Value selling is simply a focused approach on the customer; ideally, your sales force should know more about your customer than your customer does. This is a completely different mind-set from traditional selling. It requires gaining a deep understanding of your customer's problems and challenges and needs so that you can develop innovative solutions that can be sold on value. Value selling, just like Lean, can be an effective mechanism for transforming the culture of an organization. Harsco implemented value selling in two segments, and once it was fully embraced, it produced strong results.

8. Implement a Variable Cost Model

A variable cost model is crucial for enterprises that operate in cyclical markets or must invest substantial cash in capital expenditures to sustain their business. If an enterprise is exposed to both conditions, the risks are significantly amplified. These enterprises are particularly vulnerable during an economic downturn if a simultaneous and precipitous drop in pricing occurs. That's why these enterprises need a flexible and variable cost model that will allow the company to significantly and quickly reduce its costs as markets turn down. This is a vital lifeline.

All long-term contracts need to have flexibility built in so that in the event of a downturn, the company can take immediate action to reduce its costs. This reaction to economic downturns includes the ability to adjust personnel costs quickly. That's why an aversion to bricks and mortar should be entrenched in the culture of the company. If heavy investment in equipment is needed, enterprises must develop appropriate strategies to minimize the amount of fixed assets they carry on the balance sheet.

One effective mechanism is to develop strategic relationships with suppliers, agents, distributors, and even competitors that allow maximum flexibility. For example, an enterprise might develop a strategic alliance with a competitor that would allow it to rent equipment in lieu of both purchasing the same equipment. Such an alliance provides variability and reduces the need to invest precious cash resources on capital expenditures, and it ensures that the market is not flooded with equipment, particularly during a downturn.

Business models that rely on orders of short duration or situations where end-markets are unpredictable and highly cyclical must seriously consider this and other comparable options. Leaders must ensure that they adequately mitigate the risk of overinvestment in equipment, because it can potentially impair the health of the organization. The design of the business model is critical in developing an effective risk-mitigation strategy.

When designing a variable cost model, operating leverage is the key. The ability to scale the business with minimal costs contributes significantly to value creation because a major portion of every incremental dollar of revenue can flow directly to the bottom line and thus increases shareholder value. Innovative business models that are variable and scalable are not only a true lifeline, but they can also provide a sustained competitive advantage.

9. Review the Global Legal and Tax Structure

An organization's legal and tax structure needs periodic review from both an economic standpoint and a risk viewpoint. This review is particularly important if an enterprise's current structure is outdated and/or inefficient. You will need to engage outside firms to assist with this complex project. These experts will help you assess both the tax inefficiencies and the risk exposure of your organization. From a risk-mitigation viewpoint, serious consideration should be given to structuring all the business units as separate, wholly owned subsidiaries.

Under this legal structure, the parent is the holding company. Although this structure is initially burdensome from an administrative standpoint and due to one-time fees, the long-term potential protection for the enterprise is invaluable. A legal firewall is an important lifeline in today's highly litigious society. Note that this structuring could have a significant impact on the organizational structure that was discussed in chapter 4, "Business Model."

10. Develop Exceptional Project-Management Skills

Executed effectively, project management can consistently deliver projects on time and within budget. In order for projects to be properly managed and delivered successfully, the enterprise must develop powerful tools, software, procedures, and processes. All of these crucial elements must be put in the hands of a manager who has been highly trained in project management and has a history of delivering results.

Some examples of internally focused projects that require project-management skills include the start-up at a green-field site for a new plant; implementation of a new enterprise resource planning system (enterprise software); opening a new shared-services center; a major restructuring initiative; entering a new market in a foreign country; and the development of new products. Enterprises that can execute these types of projects flawlessly and consistently can create appreciable value. Note that sometimes it makes sense to outsource a project to an outside organization if the project is exceptionally complex or large in scale.

Innovation

Innovation needs to be broadly viewed as not only new products and services but also as the science, research, technology, generative thinking, processes, and business model necessary to manage the enterprise. Innovation should be the lifeblood of the organization, and it must provide a distinctive advantage. Innovation includes the next eight exceptional capabilities.

11. Focus on Brand Development

A consistently delivered positive experience by all those who interact with an enterprise is the cornerstone of a successful enterprise and the only way to build a valuable and long-lasting brand. Strong brand development begins with the CEO and flows to the employees and those who interact with customers and the community.

Brand is also built through the quality, safety, integrity, community involvement, sustainability, financial strength, design, innovation, and performance of the product, service, or solution that a company sells. Clearly, one of the branding gurus is the late CEO of Apple, Steve Jobs, who told his biographer about Mike Markkula's maxim: "A good company must impute—it must convey its values and importance in everything it does, from packaging to marketing."[68]

12. Invest in Science and Innovation

Innovative solutions for customers is the core of an organization. Innovation is your autoimmune system for fighting off the dreaded disease of commoditization. However, most enterprises cannot afford to invest massive sums of money to create and sustain a large research and development group. The good news is that you don't need to. There are now successful and effective modern models that can be benchmarked and tailored to your specific situation.

Procter & Gamble's Connect and Develop model for innovation is particularly good. Larry Huston and Nabil Sakkab wrote about this model in a 2006 *Harvard Business Review* article, and at the time it was described as a radical strategy to open innovation. Harsco implemented a similar program through our transformation innovation initiative. In 2010, with the assistance of an outside consulting firm, we successfully implemented our innovation network. By the end of 2011, we signed a record number of strategic technology agreements throughout the world.

These are technologies that we would never have known about without our innovation network. In addition to the technology agreements, we signed strategic alliances with key universities to perform very specific research in critical areas of focus for the company. The final benefit of our innovation network is that it brought together all of the in-house knowledge and expertise that was previously dispersed and uncoordinated throughout the world.

13. Design an Effective Talent-Management System

A direct correlation exists between having an exceptional talent management and leadership development capability and achieving elite status as an enterprise. An innovative talent-management system—such as those developed by General Electric, IBM, and Procter & Gamble, among others—needs to be grounded by an effective compensation system that is aligned with performance and shareholder interests. A strong link between pay and performance is essential, as is how well the system aligns with the core philosophy of the company.

An innovative talent-management and leadership-development system can provide a competitive advantage. A dynamic and best-of-class system is also usually underpinned by a healthy culture and a learning entity. There is more discussion on talent management in chapter 7, "People Excellence."

14. Monitor Sales Cadence, Backlog, and Forecasting

With continuing economic uncertainty throughout the world, a potent and innovative sales cadence, backlog, and forecasting process is an essential lifeline for all organizations. This is also highlighted in chapter 3, "Proactive Actions." For an enterprise to be managed effectively, it is imperative that an effective process is established for capturing (daily, if possible) the sales cadence.

Organizations that have timely visibility in their order flow can take positive and proactive actions, as opposed to a process that only captures order flow on a weekly or monthly basis. The sales-cadence process obviously builds the backlog. Again, no matter what the business is, all organizations should be able to compile their backlog. A backlog that contains estimated gross margins is even more effective. Ultimately, a strong sales-cadence process, along with backlog information, provides the organization with the ability to accurately forecast results. This information is one of the critical elements in scanning the environment (see next capability) so that proactive action can be taken by the enterprise to adjust its cost structure, reacting to market trends and customer needs.

15. Do a Real-Time Scan of the Environment

The ability to scan the environment in real time is an important capability that all organizations need to develop, particularly if considerable turbulence exists in the market. This ability is critical so that proactive actions can be taken by the enterprise to avoid or at least minimize the potential effect from major threats that emanate from risks and uncertainties. It is imperative for the enterprise to stay ahead of the storm. I would argue that organizations that find themselves in a difficult and challenging situation most likely did not have the right mechanisms in place to scan the environment.

Every company has certain unique real-time embedded mechanisms in place, while others are applicable to most enterprises. For example, the ability to scan what is transpiring in key end-markets, from a macro viewpoint, is usually universal. This, however, is not enough! It is essential that organizations have real-time, detailed information on trends in their specific markets and on what major customers are thinking and doing.

As discussed in the prior capability, the sales-cadence process is a vital element that functions as an early warning sign. You'll also need a powerful process in place that analyzes economic data of key countries as well as geopolitical events. This data and related assessment should be an integral part of the decision-making process of the organization, and be embedded in the planning process, the forecasting process, and the strategic road map.

16. View Information Technology as a Strategic Asset

In many organizations, the information-technology group operates mostly in a supporting role. This role usually includes implementation and maintenance of enterprise resource planning (ERP) software; infrastructure (hardware and software); mission-critical applications; and support. Although these are all necessary for operating the business, they are nonetheless mostly overhead. Information technology can and should be transformed into a strategic asset by redefining its mission.

In a 2013 article in the *Financial Times* publication *Agenda*, Tony Chapelle clearly supports this point: "Companies generate 26% higher profits than their peers when they're 'digitally mature,' which means they've fundamentally transformed their businesses through technology. That's according to a two-year study by research firm CAPgemini, which looked at 400 global corporations."[69] This point is further supported by *Fortune* in a November 18, 2013, article by Jennifer Alsever titled "Technology is the Best Policy." The article features MetLife and how they have used technology (data and software) to improve their business and change their culture.

The information-technology group mind-set needs to be completely changed to value creation so that they think differently about their role in the organization. The group needs to be challenged relative to its historical responsibilities, structure, and leadership. For example, when implementing a new ERP system, the challenge should be to arrive at a creative and value-adding solution that effectively addresses the long-term strategy of the business while providing the company with the ability to value-sell to the customer. Second, the information-technology group needs to be fully integrated into the business and be seen as a true partner. It should provide creative solutions, particularly to the frontline troops, so that they are more effective in selling value to the customer. The group needs to be led by an executive who understands digital technology and how it can positively influence the enterprise. It needs to embrace the power of apps and understand how they can improve the business and thus results. Finally, the group needs to embrace social-media technologies and utilize them effectively in the delivery of superior services and products to the customer.

For example, there are apps that can considerably improve the sales and marketing team's effectiveness. This effort should be focused in two areas: apps used while with the customer and those that reduce the administrative burden. Innovative applications that the sales and marketing team can use to demonstrate the value of the company while with the customer can sometimes be the differentiator in landing an order. With respect to the administrative burden, too often the sales and marketing teams have to spend an inordinate amount of time performing nonvalue-added administration. Smart companies that have examined this area are surprised as to how much time these teams spend away from the sales and marketing effort. Information technology can make a contribution to the enterprise by freeing up the sales and marketing team to do the most important part of their job—selling.

There are numerous other applications and innovations that a business-partner-focused information-technology group can bring to the organization to improve competitiveness. Some examples include providing effective solutions to employees who are at customer jobsites; mining customer data more effectively; and integrating applications with those of the customer so that it becomes more difficult to be dislodged by a competitor.

Leading enterprises are also employing an effective mechanism of recruiting a digital director to join the board of directors as a way to provide more focus on transforming the information-technology group. A board director with this perspective can be invaluable to the enterprise because he or she understands how this type of innovation can have a meaningful impact on the company.

17. Seek Out Joint Ventures and Strategic Alliances

Elite organizations ensure that joint ventures and strategic alliances are a core and innovative competency of the enterprise. These vehicles can be enormous value creators if they are executed well. They can also be a disaster if executed poorly.

Joint ventures and strategic alliances serve a dual purpose. They are an effective vehicle for growth and, just as importantly, they are a great mechanism for innovation. As discussed in chapter 5, "Learning Entity," they are also an effective mechanism for learning.

Developing this skill internally takes considerable time and resources. Once this capability is well developed within the organization, organic growth and innovation can be accelerated and shareholder value can be created. However, enterprises must remember my three sacrosanct rules of successful joint ventures: select the right partner, maintain control (if possible), and have a clearly defined exit strategy.

Joint ventures and strategic alliances have the potential to reduce the amount of cash investment required by an enterprise, spreading the risk while at the same time opening up new markets, particularly international ones. Considerable due diligence is required to ensure that that the venture partner adheres to similar core values and conducts business at the highest ethical standards. Use the services of your own internal security and compliance groups, those of outside firms, and publicly accessible government resources as your primary discovery resources.

The joint-venture exceptional capability is so important that I would like to share two extraordinary and successful examples.

> » During the early 1990s, there was considerable consolidation of defense assets, and we were under pressure to divest our defense business because we were a relatively small player. However, instead of selling, we smartly formed a strategic joint venture with an excellent company, FMC Corporation.

FMC was the perfect partner, and we formed the perfect joint venture. We put together a billion-dollar premier global manufacturer of track vehicles for the military. Other than the Abrams tank, we manufactured the majority of key track equipment supplying a large part of the world with such vehicles as the Bradley Fighting Vehicle, the M109 Paladin Howitzer, the M88 Recovery Vehicle, and many others.

By any measure, including economic value created, cash flow, and return on invested capital, this business was an enormous success. It was ultimately sold at a high price to a private equity group, and now it's part of a large and successful global defense group.

> » In 2008, I began an initiative to meaningfully expand our business in China. After a considerable effort in finding the right partner and negotiating an agreement, we were rewarded in 2011 with the largest contract in the history of the company (continuing operations), with an estimated value of approximately $500 million. We developed an innovative environmental solution that was enthusiastically endorsed by our partner and the Chinese government.

Our solution addressed two critical needs of the Chinese centered on the environment. The first was solving their stainless-steel slag waste stream where we were able to essentially recover 100 percent of the metal from the slag. This technology provided two benefits: it solved a waste-stream issue and it provided a low-cost source of high-value material for producing steel. The second problem we solved centers around the remaining material after the metal is recovered. Normally this material would be landfilled at a cost. Our solution substantially reduced the need to landfill, and we also developed an after-market for the material.

So waste that had been a cost burden for the customer became a revenue stream. Our innovative solution was recognized at the time by the Chinese as the first of its kind.

18. Target Strategic Acquisitions

Acquisitions can be excellent vehicles to not only grow the enterprise but also accelerate the development of technology and innovation. The acquisition process intersects with crucial elements of an enterprise's strategic core, including its envisioned future and five-year road map, and involves a host of core organizational processes and skills, such as sourcing transactions, valuation, negotiation, definitive agreement, due diligence, integration planning, and the postacquisition review of the transaction. Just as important, acquisitions should be strategically targeted and a disciplined stage-gate process followed. Enterprises that have a well-developed acquisition playbook along with strong execution abilities can create shareholder value. A strong example of such a company is Roper, which is also discussed in chapter 4, "Business Model," and chapter 8, "Distinctive Culture."

I believe acquisitions or inorganic growth must augment organic growth but should not be the focal point of growth. When acquisitions are contemplated, organizations should focus on these crucial questions in evaluating a potential target:

» Does the target company fit with the core mission statement of the enterprise?

» What is the recipe of the company, and does it have unique activities that provide a sustained competitive advantage?

» What are the innovation and intellectual-capital capabilities of the target company?

» What are the exceptional capabilities of the target company?

» What are the end-markets served, what are the short- and long-term trends of the markets, and what is the market position of the target company?

» What is the quality of the management team and the entire organization?

» What are the gross margins, operating margins, and free-cash-flow characteristics of the company?

» Will the acquisition be accretive to earnings and growth of the company both near-term and long-term?

Globalization

Globalization includes the ability to grow consistently in a disciplined manner, balancing the portfolio to minimize concentration risk and discovering opportunities in new markets. Globalization includes the last two exceptional capabilities, but as discussed earlier, both joint ventures/strategic alliances and acquisitions are an integral part of the globalization strategy. They are not repeated in the following segment since they have already been covered under "Innovation."

19. Maintain Disciplined Growth

Disciplined growth is difficult to achieve, but really successful companies avoid many of the traps and problems associated with inconsistent or erratic growth exemplified by Packard's law and the 20 Mile March, as expertly described in Jim Collins's seminal works *Good to Great* and *Great by Choice.*

Packard's law, named after the great David Packard (cofounder of Hewlett-Packard Company) states, "No company can grow revenues consistently faster than its ability to get enough of the right people to implement that growth and still become a great company. If your growth rate in revenues consistently outpaces your growth rate in people, you simply will not—indeed cannot—build a great company."[70]

The 20 Mile March is a simple but very effective concept about the importance of disciplined growth. Companies that grow in a controlled and disciplined manner typically outperform enterprises that grow erratically. The 20 Mile March "requires hitting specified performance markers with great consistency over a long period of time. It requires two distinct types of discomfort, delivering high performance in difficult times and holding back in good times."[71]

Although it is a relatively easy concept to understand, it takes a considerable effort to arrive at the correct answer. In Harsco's case, we ultimately settled on consistent EVA growth as our 20 Mile March. Because we were an EVA company and value creation was also a core value, we came to the realization that this one metric best represented the path forward to long-term shareholder value. By generating positive

EVA growth every year—say, consistently for twenty years—the value created would obviously be positive. The amount of value creation would of course depend on the cumulative value of all EVA created plus the expected future growth of EVA.

20. Identify Frontier Markets

The final exceptional capability is finding new areas for profitable growth—that is, where can the business create incremental value in the future by investing in areas that perhaps competitors are not seeing? For example, Harsco started a process to internally identify the "next UAE." Where is the next market or markets that offer significant upside potential for our strongly positioned businesses? This initiative requires generative thinking, considerable dialogue, and due diligence. It also requires you to be close to the customer, because customers can provide valuable information and intelligence on various markets.

What is important in the process, however, is to not make large bets. The approach must be to make many smaller bets to test various frontier markets that improve performance without taking outsized risks.

Lifelines Inventory

It is particularly important for all enterprises to know exactly what lifelines they have before embarking on any major journey. When mountaineers prepare for a climb, they know exactly what they have in terms of information on the weather, team, supplies, capabilities, and other mission critical needs. Enterprises need to do the same.

Just as it is necessary to take an inventory of all of our personal lifelines, it is just as important to catalogue all of the enterprise lifelines. This detailed examination and assessment of vital lifelines should be done urgently in order to determine what areas the company needs to improve on. Here is a framework to follow:

» The inventory and related honest assessment should be completed periodically, at least annually.

» A disciplined process should be followed.

» The process should include the involvement of the global leadership team and possibly the board of directors in identifying and assessing strengths and weaknesses.

» Involvement of an outside firm to assist with the assessment and possibly with the implementation should be considered.

» The inventory should result in a detailed action plan that addresses shortfalls. The action plan should be incorporated into the strategic road map.

» Appropriate metrics should be implemented to ensure progress is measured.

Takeaways

In this chapter you learned about the twenty exceptional capabilities necessary to build a successful enterprise. Well-executed capabilities can materially improve the performance of the enterprise and create meaningful value. Without these exceptional skills, it is difficult, if not impossible, for a company to reach elite status.

It is essential that each exceptional capability be designed and developed in a balanced and efficient way. Consistent flawless execution of the capabilities—which can be divided into the three philosophical strategies of optimization, innovation, and globalization—provides a competitive advantage and can notably differentiate a company in the marketplace.

CHAPTER 7

People Excellence

The As are people who are filled with passion, committed
to making things happen, open to ideas from anywhere,
and blessed with lots of runway ahead of them.
—Jack Welch[72]

Selecting the right people can make the difference between
excellence and mediocrity. It can also be the difference between success
and failure. A strong example of selecting the right people can be found
in Stephen Ambrose's book *Undaunted Courage*, which is the incredible
account of the Lewis and Clark expedition. President Thomas Jefferson
selected Captain Meriwether Lewis to lead an audacious journey up the
Missouri River, over the Rocky Mountains, down the Columbia River,
and ultimately to the Pacific Ocean.[73]

President Jefferson did not rely on luck or advice from others in making
his selection. He chose Captain Lewis to lead the expedition because he
knew the man and his abilities. Lewis had just spent two years living
with the president as his secretary. Thus, after years of working closely
with Captain Lewis along with many years of observing his development
and personal precocious characteristics, Jefferson was able to choose the

right leader for this important journey. Captain Lewis followed a similar approach as the president in selecting his cocommander, William Clark. Lewis had served under Clark and knew of his strong characteristics and abilities. When it comes to the selection of excellent people, leaders cannot get this wrong. President Jefferson knew this, Captain Lewis knew it also, and, as I will explain in this chapter, you must know it as well.

Building a Strong Foundation

People Excellence is the first of three essential foundational lifelines that all elite, enduring enterprises share. The other two underlying lifelines are explored in chapter 8, "Distinctive Culture," and chapter 9, "Core Philosophy." In my view, without a strong foundation, sustainable superior performance is not possible.

In the book *Extreme Alpinism: Climbing Light, Fast, and High*, authors Mark F. Twight and James Martin highlight the importance of building a strong foundation before commencing any ascent to the summit. "If you're starting with little or no foundation … to alpine climbing, your first training must address the sheer volume of work involved in ascending a mountain," the authors note. "Begin your training program with that magnitude of effort in mind. … Building a foundation takes time. … Once an adequate … foundation has been developed, it's time to move ahead into specific training for strength and for endurance in the mountains."[74]

People Excellence

No matter how talented its leader, without the help of an A-team at the top, the enterprise is unlikely to thrive—and might just fail. The late CEO of Apple, Steve Jobs, was reportedly fanatical about fielding a world-class A-team. That's one of the reasons I believe Jobs was such an exceptional CEO, perhaps one of the best in history. He refused to accept even one B-player because he knew that a direct correlation exists between talent and results. Of course, even Jobs and his proven management style were not invincible and immune to the impact of an unprecedented string of bad-luck events that might have rendered him and his team powerless to change. Still, the logic of a top-notch A-player is undeniable and the best insurance against even such an unlikely set of poor luck-spread circumstances.

Much has been written on the subject of acquiring A-players, so this chapter will examine the topic from a slightly different perspective through

» a discussion of the key personal leadership characteristics members of the A-team must possess;

» an exploration of the absolutely fundamental role played by a powerful internal talent-management and leadership-development process in building a pool of potential A-team members and why such investments are imperative; and

» a frank discussion of why outside recruitment (particularly for senior management positions) is fraught with risks, and why luck plays a role in the ultimate success of any enterprise strategy.

The Right People

The old adage that "people are our most important asset" is only half-true. In reality, the *right* people are an enterprise's most important asset. In his diagnostic tool *Where Are You on Your Journey from Good to Great?*, Jim Collins notes that "those who build great organizations make sure they have the right people on the bus, the wrong people off the bus, and the right people in the key seats before they figure out where to drive the bus."[75]

So who are the right people? That's what the next section explores.

Nine Critical "Right People" Personal Characteristics

First, it is essential that the leadership team is unified around a mission and a set of values that are ultimately manifested in the personal characteristics of the team. At Harsco, a total of nine characteristics were identified that all seventy-five members of the key-seats leadership team needed to possess to be part of this distinguished group. A much larger group called the global leadership team was comprised of these top executives plus about 175 additional officers and key middle managers. To be on the larger global leadership team, prospective members had to demonstrate three distinctive characteristics that we believed would contribute to building an enterprise destined to last for generations:

1. Integrity and ethics
2. A willingness to be a team player
3. An ability to consistently deliver high results

These criteria are the glue that holds a team together across the world, and as such they are the characteristics that always should be self-evident no matter where or when a team member interacts with anyone in the company. We incorporated these three characteristics into our core mission statement (or purpose) in order to highlight their importance.

Six additional characteristics were defined as important and essential for the key-seats leadership team. Key-seats members must demonstrate:

4. A good fit with core values
5. An ability to self-manage with minimal guidance
6. An understanding and acceptance of their responsibilities
7. Consistency and follow-through in what they say and do
8. Acceptance of responsibility and accountability for their actions, including giving appropriate credit to others for success
9. Passion for and pride in the company's culture

All individuals on the key-seats leadership team had to clear the high bar set by these nine characteristics. Here are some more details about each characteristic and why it was chosen for the list:

1. *Integrity and ethics.* Clearly, maintaining high social, ethical, and organizational standards is a baseline requirement for any team member. For Harsco, this designated someone who conformed to the company's code of conduct and was relentless in establishing, developing, and continuously improving safety practices. To

paraphrase what I pointed out in an earlier chapter, the most basic requirement for any enterprise member starts and ends with integrity.

2. *A willingness to be a team player.* This characteristic was consistent with Harsco's core philosophy. It is fairly easy to identify a team player. A team player is someone who participates with others to accomplish the goals of the enterprise and displays total alignment with the enterprise's strategy and purpose. Here's a simple self-assessment on this characteristic. Ask yourself, "Am I someone who consistently puts the success of the team above my own interests?" We chose this as our second characteristic to demonstrate the importance of teams working together across the world, as outlined in Harsco's mission statement. Without it, we strongly believed Harsco's business model would not be effective.

3. *An ability to consistently deliver high results.* Someone who consistently gets things done and delivers on promises—and even exceeds them—was considered a high-results-oriented team member. These individuals characteristically didn't overpromise and never intentionally sandbagged any commitment. Note that we acknowledged that it was easy to identify potential internal team members who manifested this characteristic but almost impossible to consistently assess and identify this characteristic when recruiting a team member from the outside.

4. *A good fit with core values.* Team members needed to display passion for Harsco's four core values of integrity, people, continuous improvement, and value creation. Assessing each member's daily adherence and passion for each of these core values proved to be challenging, as explained in chapter 5, "Learning Entity." Here are some basic questions to ask yourself when assessing these values: How does the team member manifest passion for the core values? How is each core value adhered to by the team member? What effective mechanisms have been established to embed the core values in the culture of the company? Do these mechanisms

have teeth? What metrics have been established to meaningfully measure adherence and passion to the core values?

5. *An ability to self-manage with minimal guidance.* The right people are usually self-motivated and self-disciplined. That's why bureaucracy and other suffocating policies and procedures need to be minimized so that people are allowed to operate within a framework that promotes creativity and productivity and brings the best out in individuals. Again, this is a very difficult characteristic to properly assess.

6. *An understanding and acceptance of their responsibilities.* The sixth characteristic relates closely to the one before it. The right people understand the difference between simply having a job and being responsible and accountable. Individuals who possess this characteristic understand that they have an immense amount of freedom to innovate, achieve results, and contribute to the overall success of the enterprise.

7. *Consistency and follow-through in what they say and do.* The next characteristic relates very closely to characteristic number 3, and it thus should be assessed at the same time. Disciplined people are always careful of their commitments, and so they consistently fulfill their promises. They practice extreme commitment to the cause.

8. *Acceptance of responsibility and accountability for their actions, including giving appropriate credit to others for success.* These individuals have the courage to confront reality, accept the truth, and value a culture of substance, integrity, and results. They accept responsibility when things go wrong, and they give credit to others when things go well. They also conduct intense dialogues and debates in search of best answers and are utterly intolerant of mediocrity. Importantly, these individuals cultivate other leaders who possess these characteristics.

9. *Passion for and pride in the company's culture.* These individuals promote the brand and demonstrate a fierce resolve to adhering to the core values. They promote with passion the culture of the company. This characteristic is closely linked to number 4.

Additional Key Characteristics

What is not specifically identified in the nine characteristics are some other essential elements that need to be either added or combined with the base nine. These additional characteristics include the following:

» strong communication skills, which are absolutely critical today in a business world that is so competitive and so customer-centric

» quality-thinking or critical-thinking capabilities, which are quite different from just having pure intellect—they take discipline, experience, perspective, common sense, and judgment

» loyalty that is not just blind acceptance of everything the CEO says and does, but a determination not to undermine the CEO or peers in the organization

Defining the Global Leadership Team and the Key-Seats Leadership Team

In early 2008, with the nine people characteristics defined and our core philosophy codified and enunciated, Harsco undertook the task of defining the Harsco global leadership team and the key-seats leadership team. By benchmarking with another company, we developed a framework that was effective for our organization and fit well with our human-capital processes and technology infrastructure.

We first defined the main Harsco global leadership team, which consisted of about 250 people. We arrived at this number by taking all the direct reports to the CEO and their direct reports two levels down in the organization chart. Members of the key-seats leadership team, about seventy-five in all, were direct reports to the CEO and included most of their direct reports one level down. We put these seats in an organization-chart format using PowerPoint and color-coded all seats as either green or red. Also, all members of the key-seats leadership team were identified by a double border around the box.

If a box was green, that meant the right person was in the right seat and no action was necessary. A red box, however, meant one of five things:

an open recruitment was underway for the position; the member was retiring within the next twelve months; the person was in the wrong seat; the wrong person was on the bus; or the individual was on a development plan. We also developed metrics around the leadership team—mainly the percentage of key seats filled by the right people. Our target was at least 90 percent. Visually, this was an effective tool. With a quick scan, an executive was able to see the entire organization, including the key-seats leadership team, and recognize which positions required action.

We tied succession planning to this as well. We would review the leadership team with the board at least annually, but generally more frequently. We also began to take this to a much higher level. We started weekly key-seats assessments. We also started developing better tools so that we could capture more complete information on each person. My goal was to create an app that fully automated the profile of each key seat so that managers, no matter where they were in the world, would be able to instantly view their organization with a simple click or touch of a screen. More importantly, we started thinking about how to better measure each individual against the three characteristics and the nine characteristics. Our long-term goal was to implement a fully integrated and interactive global human-capital framework to drive our talent-management and leadership-development strategy, similar to popular social-media technology.

Not every company can afford to spend millions of dollars implementing a global system for human-capital talent management and leadership development. I believe you can be thrifty and yet have an efficient and effective tool to manage your most important asset, your people. This can be accomplished by implementing basic low-cost ideas from other companies. One idea is to use the PowerPoint color-coded evaluation and succession-planning system that we developed. Also, there are numerous low-cost tools available for assessing people. Work with a corporate psychologist and benchmark with other organizations so that you develop an effective array of tools. This can provide the bridge for a company that needs to get control of its human-capital framework but does not have sufficient resources. What is important is to be proactive.

Alternative Framework for Assessing
Personal Characteristics

An alternative and more effective approach to the nine personal characteristics for the key-seats leadership team is to vigorously assess the thirty precocious characteristics that are discussed in chapter 1. The thirty precocious characteristics are all-encompassing and should be used to measure crucial qualities of each key-seat member, including the following:

» depth of integrity, perspective, passion, courage, wisdom, and generative thinking

» ability to learn and grow individually and to help others develop

» level of participation in the organization and the community

» value-creation contribution to the long-term health of the organization

» consistent demonstration of discipline, humility, loyalty, accountability, and equanimity

» emotional maturity and common sense

» proactive mind-set and ability to get things done

» ability to navigate and survive major global shocks and unforeseen challenges

» effective manifestation of instinct

This framework can also be used by the board of directors in assessing both the CEO and his identified potential successors. The assessment and development of these characteristics should be embedded into the talent-management and leadership-development process, and it must be overseen by trained experts. To paraphrase what I said in chapter 1, the strength and quality of the thirty precocious characteristics will ultimately determine the success of a leader and the business he or she leads.

Innovative Talent-Management and Leadership-Development Practice

The leading global companies all share one common element: they have a well-developed and well-funded talent-management and leadership-development practice. I believe that an innovative practice can consistently produce A-players, and it can provide the enterprise with a sustainable, competitive advantage. However, not all enterprises have the resources or the commitment to match proportionally what the top-tier or elite companies invest in recruiting, developing, and retaining their people. The good news is that you don't need to spend vast sums to implement an effective talent-management and leadership-development system. What is important is that you have one and that you focus on continuous improvement. The talent-management process should be at the forefront of the CEO, senior management, and board of directors' radar. Companies that do not focus on this are doomed to mediocrity or even failure.

One company that has excelled at talent management is General Electric (GE). In the book *Jack: Straight from the Gut*, Jack Welch does a wonderful job of recounting how GE approached talent management. Welch devotes a chapter to people, and here is how he segmented his teams:

> The As are people who are filled with passion, committed to making things happen, open to ideas from anywhere, and blessed with lots of runway ahead of them. They have the ability to energize not only themselves, but everyone who comes in contact with them. They make business productive and fun at the same time … It's this passion, probably more than anything else, that separates the As from the Bs. The Bs are the heart of the company and are critical to its operational success. We devote lots of energy toward improving the Bs. We want them to search every day for what they're missing to become As. The manager's job is to help them get there. The C player is someone who can't get the job done. Cs are likely to enervate rather than energize. They procrastinate rather than deliver …[76]

In addition to defining the various people categories, Welch provides details on the tools GE used to evaluate people and how the reward system was aligned with the rankings. He also provides insight on what they did with the C-players. Although GE's process of forced evaluations is now out of favor with many companies (according to a November 2013 *Wall Street Journal* article),[77] I believe that the main principle of identifying and segmenting team members is still valid. What is important is what the company does with the information once it's compiled.

I recommend that C-players be closely assessed to ensure that they are not simply in the wrong position or in need of more development. Do not easily give up on employees. There are, of course, always a certain number of employees who need to be encouraged to pursue a career elsewhere. Furthermore, I believe that enterprises that vigorously implement the learning lifeline as discussed in chapter 5, "Learning Entity," will have more success in developing team members.

Promote from Within for Senior Management

Earlier in chapter 5, "Learning Entity," the topic of promoting and developing internal talent versus recruiting senior management from the outside was explained in some detail. The main point to reiterate is that in the long run, better results are achieved and costs are reduced by developing and grooming future management from the inside. Bringing talent in from the outside, particularly at the senior management level, is fraught with risks, including potential negative effects on the culture of the company. It is like rolling the dice in gambling; sometimes you are lucky and win, but most of the time you lose. For example, IBM was lucky in hiring Louis V. Gerstner Jr., but he is more the exception than the rule.

A May 2012 *Wall Street Journal* article by Rachel Emma Silverman and Lauren Weber strongly supports this promote-from-within philosophy. The authors point out that "promoting from within—from the CEO on down—can deliver more benefits for companies than hiring outside talent, a growing body of research suggests." The authors also point to a recent study from the University of Pennsylvania Wharton School that "found that external hires were paid some 18 percent more than internal employees in equivalent roles, but fared worse in performance reviews during their first two years on the job."[78]

A September 2012 article in *Fortune* about hiring makes the point entirely clear. The article title and subtitle say it all: "Avoid Hiring the Unexpected: A good employee is hard to find—even in the age of *Facebook* and *LinkedIn*. Vetting for the top spot can be especially tough. Why reference checks fail, and how they can be fixed."[79]

If you think about this issue pragmatically, how can you truly assess a person just by a resume, a couple of interviews, and references that are for the most part staged? I would argue you can't! People can only be adequately assessed through years of working closely with them and seeing how they perform as they pass through the company's development program, including stretch assignments.

Takeaways

In this chapter, we note that the right people are your lifeline. An innovative and exceptional talent-management and leadership-development practice can be a differentiator. Investing in this practice is the responsibility of every CEO, and the board of directors must also be fully engaged. Selecting, developing, and retaining the right team is the most important responsibility of a CEO. All leaders must simply get this right. The board of directors must also be an integral part of this process, because they are ultimately responsible for the CEO.

Define the structure and values of the organization. Invest in the human capital framework of the organization. Develop talent and assess high-potential individuals over a period of time to ensure that they are the right people. Avoid filling senior management positions, including the CEO, from outside the organization. Embed the requisite qualities in the organization by implementing the appropriate mechanism. Adopt low-cost ideas on how to better manage your most important asset. Internet-based systems and other internally developed programs can allow companies to more effectively manage their human-capital resources.

You need to be consistent and disciplined in people decisions. Focus on establishing the personal characteristics that are most aligned with the core philosophy of the company. A recommended approach for the key-seats leadership team is to use the thirty precocious characteristics. Establish the appropriate processes, metrics, and mechanisms to ensure these personal qualities are properly assessed.

If you do need to recruit from the outside, hire around the core philosophy of the enterprise and the indispensable personal characteristics. Implement a robust hiring process and involve key seats on the search team. Finally, do not rush the decision. Take your time and make sure that the person who is ultimately hired possesses all the qualities that are necessary for the organization to advance and fulfill its core mission.

CHAPTER 8

Distinctive Culture

Changing culture is not a sprint. It's a marathon.
It's very, very hard to affect culture.
—Carol Bartz[80]

Establishing a distinctive culture is one of the most essential organizational lifelines. While many CEOs and well-regarded business leaders might argue a different priority—sustainable growth or perhaps innovative practices—I contend if for no other reason than common sense alone that culture deserves to be near the top of the lifelines list.

To put this discussion in terms of the central mountain-climbing metaphor for this book, the climbing code cited in the book *Mountaineering: The Freedom of the Hills* offers a close parallel and highlights the importance of culture:

> Mountaineers devised a set of guidelines to help people conduct themselves safely in the mountains. Based on careful observation of the habits of skilled climbers and a thoughtful analysis of accidents, those guidelines have served well ... climbing code is built on the premise that

mountaineers want a high probability for safety and success, even in risk-filled or doubtful situations, and that they want an adequate margin of safety in case they have misjudged their circumstance.[81]

The focus of this chapter will be to examine the importance of culture and the five essential elements for creating a distinctive culture. Broadly viewed, culture is simply the way people connect with each other, the way they behave and think, and the way they commit to the core philosophy and business model of the organization.

CEO Perspective on Culture

Louis V. Gerstner Jr., the exceptional 1990s-era IBM CEO, relied on shifting the organization's culture to drive the success of the business transformation he headed for the company. In fact, in recalling his experiences during the reinvention of IBM, he stated that "culture isn't just one aspect of the game—it is the game."[82] This view was strongly reinforced by another outstanding CEO, Fred Hassan, who said, "transformations do not occur without culture change … Strong cultures are characterized by strong convergence and alignment around vision, mission, values, and strategic direction. Changing culture starts by changing attitudes and behaviors."[83]

I have a different idea as to why such a high lifeline ranking is a common-sense and even a practical-experience conclusion. Even if your only reference point is your own family or the family of a friend or colleague, you know that a dysfunctional or disharmonious home culture is usually manifested by infighting, backstabbing, stress, distraction, and unhappiness. So why would we think a dysfunctional or disharmonious organizational culture would produce any result less destructive to unity and positive results? It's a point made by many leadership and organizational gurus, including *Good to Great* author Jim Collins.

Culture of Discipline

Both of Collins's most well-known books, *Good to Great* and *Great by Choice*, point to the importance of organizational culture and specifically to what Collins calls a *culture of discipline* that starts with basic, fundamental practices and beliefs. In his diagnostic tool *Where Are You on Your Journey from Good to Great?*, Collins states that "disciplined people who engage in disciplined thought and who take disciplined action— operating with freedom within a framework of responsibilities—this is the cornerstone of a culture that creates greatness."[84] So how do you put this point of view into organizational practice? Here are four distinctive suggestions concerning culture derived from Collins's statement.

1. Focus on your business model and never seek growth for growth's sake. Growth needs to be disciplined and well calibrated and consistent with what you do well. It also means a willingness to divest lines of businesses when it is clear you cannot be in the top tier.

2. Build a system within a framework that supports a shared sense of freedom, responsibility, and accountability. Within this widely defined framework, all employees and key stakeholders must understand they have the freedom to innovate, achieve results, and contribute to the success of the enterprise.

3. Focus on managing the system and not the people in it. That is, you should provide an environment that does not demotivate the most self-motivated and self-disciplined people. The system should help you motivate and promote the best workers. Don't impose unnecessary rules and bureaucracy that hamper the performance of the right people—they do not need a lot of rules. At the same time, you must ensure that everyone understands that with freedom comes responsibility and certain obligations, and that abuse of their independence and trust will not be tolerated. As former US Secretary of the Treasury William E. Simon once said, "Freedom is strangely ephemeral. It is something like breathing; one only becomes acutely aware of its importance when one is choking."[85]

4. In a culture of discipline, there's extreme commitment; the right people go to extremes to fulfill their commitments. These committed individuals clearly understand what President Abraham Lincoln once said: "Commitment is what transforms a promise into reality."[86]

Key Elements of a Distinctive Culture

I believe that five elements make up a strong culture. They coalesce around core mission and values, character, business model, organizational leaders, and effective mechanisms. A recent paper prepared by Booz & Company on lessons for new CEOs concluded, "Leaders typically think of culture as synonymous with values. But it's more useful to think of it as information, influence, and insights that flow among peers. Whether you have a strong or weak culture often depends on the strength and caliber of these peer connections."[87] While I agree with that, I also believe there is more to a strong culture, so I've provided further explanation of my five elements that are necessary to create a vibrant, unified, and healthy culture below:

1. *Core mission and underpinning values.* How an organization's core mission philosophy and values are embraced and embedded in the organization forms the foundation of a healthy sustainable culture and is its absolute cornerstone.

2. *Character of the right people.* Developing and hiring the right people who are passionate about the core philosophy of the organization and disciplined in thought, word, and deed is essential. These individuals clearly understand that they are accountable and responsible, and that they must consistently deliver what they promise without distraction.

3. *The right business model.* The processes and business model must allow for a free flow of exchange, interaction, and connectivity. The ability to connect and collaborate is paramount and is critical to the building of an exceptional inward and outwardly focused (i.e., on the customer) and sustainable culture.

4. *Leader excellence.* Do the leaders walk the talk? Is every action they take an example of integrity, teamwork, safety, customer service, accountability, excellence, and other relevant and essential qualities?

5. *Effective mechanisms.* In order to build and sustain a strong culture, it is essential to implement and embed mechanisms that

have teeth. For example, we started with an effective mechanism that was in place for decades, which was our "no exceptions" policy for violations of the company's sacrosanct code of conduct. We built off this strong foundation by implementing many of the mechanisms that are discussed throughout this chapter.

Unfortunately, some companies have multiple cultures, and in certain cases these companies are hampered by a dysfunctional or disharmonious culture as well. No company intentionally tries to create multiple cultures or a dysfunctional culture or a disharmonious culture, it just happens naturally over time—decades—and for a multitude of reasons, including a focus on other strategic initiatives. My own experiences, of course, form my opinions and biases toward the importance of managing culture. As CEO of Harsco, I was focused on directing that company's cultural alignment, and I believe my own experience offers some key insight for other leaders.

Harsco's Culture: The Beginning

Since its founding in 1853 in Harrisburg, Pennsylvania, Harsco has reinvented itself extremely well over the decades mainly through modern-day acquisitions and divestitures. The company was once heavily invested in the defense industry and at one time almost entirely a manufacturing business, making everything from plastic pipe to forgings to fabricated steel. All my predecessors at Harsco did a superb job of reinventing the company.

Because of the multitude of global acquisitions over many decades, numerous cultures naturally continued along with the newly acquired lines of business platforms. The result was that no unified Harsco culture existed per se. Rather, the company's culture was a collection of many cultures.

As I traveled around the world visiting the operations when I was appointed president, I realized the potential implications of such a multicultural organization. Not that multiple cultures are necessarily bad, but I believe that the culture needs to mirror the business model. Thus, it was my view at the time that a common, unified culture was required to effectively and successfully complete the business transformation journey that we were beginning, which included the strategic initiatives of optimization (OneHarsco), innovation, and globalization. This is further discussed in appendix 1, "Climb the Summit—Harsco's Journey."

The business-transformation initiative became a high-priority item with me because of my intuition or instincts that storm clouds were starting to develop. At the time, I sensed that a shift was occurring in the macroeconomic environment and in some of our key markets. This shift was occurring because of key markers that were starting to emerge. Although I did not possess unimpeachable facts to supplement my sixth sense, there were enough macroeconomic markers to cause worry. So I outlined and communicated these markers (e.g., extent of possible adverse effects from the US subprime debacle, a possible recession looming in the United States, and the concern about significantly increasing oil prices), along with suggested countermeasures, to the entire organization as soon as I officially took over as CEO on January 1, 2008.

Because of these concerns, I believed it was necessary to immediately begin preparing for the inevitable storm. Another sixth-sense conclusion at the time was that I feared Harsco's strong growth performance, particularly from 2005 through 2007, would be difficult to sustain because of two major positive factors during these years that could just as easily turn and work against our performance in the event of an extreme downturn in the business environment.

The first factor was a perfect global economic environment during this period. Every major economy in the world grew. The favorable pricing environment boosted operating results for most companies. It was my sense that the economic boom could not be sustained indefinitely (due to normal economic cycles) and that an economic calamity in the future was inevitable. I just didn't realize that the economic perfect storm would arrive so soon, and with such severity, and that it would last so long. No one could have predicted the material adverse global economic impact of the US financial crisis and later the European sovereign debt crisis.

The second factor was the devaluation of the US dollar. Approximately 70 percent of our business was outside the United States, and this meant that the translation of foreign sales and income increased when the dollar was lower than the foreign currencies in which we did business. Thus sales and income grew just from the translation effect. Again, just like the economic boom, it was my view that exchange rates would ultimately change based on historical precedent.

During the fall of 2007, I was contemplating how to meaningfully create a unified and sustainable culture under the OneHarsco optimization initiative. On a business trip that fall, I remembered how much I had enjoyed reading Jim Collins's book *Good to Great* and thought his model might provide the answer I was seeking to help transform Harsco. It was a decision that ultimately resulted in a visit to Jim Collins's lab in Boulder, Colorado.

A lab visit at the time meant that you traveled to Colorado with a maximum of eleven people and you met with Collins for approximately two half-days. The first day usually lasted from about eight in the morning until around one in the afternoon. Team homework assignments were given that took all afternoon through the early evening or later. The second half-day meeting was set aside for reviewing results and other matters. It was this process that ultimately developed a framework for unifying our culture.

Further Meetings

Prior to this initial meeting, Collins said he wanted to explore certain topics and asked me to join him and his other invitees for a separate *Good to Great* dialogue session with nine other business leaders. He not only agreed to host the Harsco senior management team but he also invited me to attend a separate dialogue session before the Harsco visit. Consequently, I was fortunate to spend two days with Collins and nine other talented leaders in early February 2008 (see chapter 3, "Proactive Actions"). This session, which is acknowledged by Jim Collins in his book *Great by Choice*, is clearly one of the most memorable moments of my business career, and it also created a useful career lifeline. During this visit, Collins gave each attendee a copy of his manuscript for the book *How the Mighty Fall* and asked us to provide comments. Again, we were all acknowledged in his book.

In March 2008, our senior management team traveled to Boulder to codify our core philosophy, work on our human-capital framework structure, envision the future, and develop several other important principles.

When we returned from Boulder, we worked for several months on putting together what we called the Harsco "Good to Great" framework. We published a booklet titled *Climb the Summit: Harsco's Ascent from Good to Great*. We used the booklet for training, orientation, and customer relations. It was a particularly good recruiting tool for the organization. We also did a video that was distributed globally, and I traveled extensively that year to many of our sites and personally taught the classes on the framework.

Key metrics were also developed to monitor our framework progress. One of the most important metrics was the number of key seats filled with the right people. We established criteria of 90 percent, as mentioned in chapter 7, "People Excellence." In addition, we established metrics over each of our four core values of integrity, people, continuous improvement, and value creation.

We put a particular emphasis on our core philosophy by inserting a statement at the beginning of every presentation and having the presenter tell an anecdote about his or her experience around the core philosophy. Sitting in meetings over the years, I took considerable pride in the compelling stories I heard, and these narratives turned out to be an effective mechanism for embedding the OneHarsco culture in the company.

We established an executive leadership team, which was made up of my senior direct reports. The team met weekly for a couple of hours. In addition to discussing and acting on daily operating issues, we devoted some portion of the meeting to culture and people. As was discussed in chapter 7, "People Excellence," we also established the key-seats leadership team and the global leadership team.

Significantly, we decided to rebrand the entire company as Harsco. We believed that the rebranding would assist in unifying the culture and connecting the company across the world. We modernized the Harsco logo and in fact used the *A* in Harsco to incorporate the climb-the-summit journey. If you look closely at the horizontal line in the capital *A* of Harsco, you will actually see a summit. And finally, we moved key executives to the headquarters office in Harrisburg. With the rebranding of the company, the implementation of the framework, and the consolidation of key executives in one location, we were on our way to creating a foundation for a unified company culture under the OneHarsco umbrella.

All these mechanisms we created to build the foundation for the OneHarsco initiative were effective to varying degrees, but ultimately a unified culture is built around a strict adherence to the five elements mentioned previously, particularly the right people on the team and choosing the right leaders. Without the alignment of all these elements, no matter how hard you try, you will lose the culture war. My experience here is that it starts and stops with the people. If you are unsuccessful in getting the right people in the right seats, the culture war may be lost along with a critical lifeline.

Distinctive Culture Examples

Reading annual reports (particularly the chairman and CEO letter) and other public company documents (particularly the 10-K and proxy statement) and other publicly facing communications, you can find some excellent examples of companies whose distinctive culture underpins their success. Two remarkable companies to consider based on such a review are RPM and Roper.

RPM was founded in 1947 and is a world leader in specialty coatings, sealants, building products, and related services, serving both industrial and consumer markets. It is also a company whose foundation is built on its culture. According to the company's publicly facing documents, the culture is built around the Value of 168:

> The Value of 168 is a statement of the corporate philosophy of RPM. This figure, often cited by our founder, Frank C. Sullivan, literally represents the number of hours in a week. On a deeper level, it serves to remind us of his belief that we are born with two great gifts: life and the time to do something with it. The Value of 168 signifies enduring commitment to our fellow employees, customers and shareholders.

This strong foundation is augmented by an entrepreneurial-culture bias toward a philosophy that states, "Hire the best people you can find. Create an atmosphere that will keep them. Then, let them do their jobs."[88] I found this statement to be extremely powerful and visionary. In fact, I believe that this is, in essence, the cornerstone of the *Good to Great* book: a culture of discipline. Certainly, the company's founder in 1947 was extraordinarily prescient.

Roper was first listed on the American Stock Exchange in 1992. It is a diversified growth company as opposed to a diversified industrial. This is an important distinction. Roper provides engineered products and solutions that create global leadership positions across a diverse set of niche markets, including software information networks, medical, water, energy, and transportation. Roper's business culture, which can be found in its annual report,

> is based on the principle that Simple Ideas and Nimble Execution produce Powerful Results in our businesses. This culture has proven as scalable as we always believed it would be. Further, our leaders continue to demonstrate an intricate understanding of their businesses, while adhering to and executing our compelling cash performance disciplines. This powerful combination of clear focus, proven strategy, and disciplined principles has created solid growth platforms at Roper.

Roper's culture is driven by cash return on invested capital. The company's focus is on the belief that "the disciplined deployment of cash flow, both organically and into high-value acquisitions, creates substantial shareholder value over time." Roper has consistently maintained "an unwavering focus on cash flow." This fanatical focus has paid off handsomely because the company's results are amazing.[89]

RPM and Roper are both elite companies. They have outperformed the S&P index for the past ten years (through 2012). Their results prove that getting the right culture and recipe in an organization can generate powerful returns. As leaders, there's much that we can all learn from these two marvelous companies.

Takeaways

A distinctive and healthy culture is the underpinning lifeline of a company. A company that has a dysfunctional or disharmonious culture will most likely not perform as well over a long horizon. Nonetheless, all good leaders should understand the importance of having a strong, unified culture where everyone is aligned, disciplined, and focused on the five core elements of culture. There can be no deviation. An organization must win the culture war before it can thrive as an enduring enterprise.

Ultimately, a strong and harmonious culture is driven by core mission and values, high-quality people, an innovative business model, and the right leadership. In a productive and healthy culture, you will also find that a number of important mechanisms have been implemented to ensure that a strong culture is embedded and sustained. Furthermore, the business model and processes lend themselves to a connecting and collaborating environment that allows employees to flourish. It is my belief, based on a number of companies I have studied, that organizations that have established a strong and healthy culture usually outperform their peers.

CHAPTER 9

Core Philosophy

The authenticity *of the ideology and the extent to which a*
company attains consistent alignment with the ideology
counts more than the content *of the ideology.*
—*Jim Collins and Jerry Porras*[90]

As companies strive to achieve excellence, leaders have a steep
mountain to climb in order to take their organizations to these new
heights. Just as mountaineers face many challenges in their climb, so do
business leaders. It is imperative that both mountaineers and business
leaders plan and think generatively about the climb and all the potential
for unpredictable weather, extreme climbing conditions, and team
performance under various difficult and challenging scenarios.

A core philosophy is part of a company's vision framework, along
with an envisioned future that looks out about twenty years. As explained
throughout this book, a core philosophy is also an integral part of the
lifelines tool kit that CEOs need in order to successfully climb the summit.
A core philosophy is built around an enterprise's mission statement and
core values and is the true heart and soul of any organization. Without
this core philosophy firmly in place, building a successful and long-lasting

enterprise is impossible. That's why I built the last five enterprise lifelines upon this strongly held belief. Based on the myriad of organizations that I have studied, I believe that there is some confusion around what a true mission statement is and what core values are. My objective with this chapter is to provide organizations with clarity and guidance on this important lifeline.

This chapter focuses on creating the crucial mission statement and the underpinning core values (or core beliefs) that ultimately drive all actions of the organization. This detailed examination begins with a review of the groundbreaking and insightful work of Jim Collins and Jerry Porras, as outlined in *Built to Last* and referred to as a *core ideology*. Then I will share a core philosophy review of three very different companies: a technology company, IBM; my own company that I recently started; and an industrial company, Harsco. I'll also provide a listing of strong mission-statement examples and review some recommended statements of core values.

Core Ideology and *Built to Last*

The classic 1994 management book by Jim Collins and Jerry Porras, *Built to Last,* brought widespread awareness of the concept of core ideology and envisioned future. Two years later, the authors published an amazing article in the *Harvard Business Review*, "Building Your Company's Vision," that provided further valuable insight and guidance into the idea of a core ideology or philosophy.

Collins and Porras define a core ideology as

> a company's timeless character. It is the glue that holds the enterprise together even when everything else is up for grabs. Core ideology is something you discover— by looking inside. It's not something you can invent, much less fake. A core ideology has two parts: (1) Core values are the handful of guiding principles by which a company navigates. (2) Core purpose is an organization's most fundamental reason for being.[91]

It is important to note that Collins and Porras make it clear that a company's core ideology and core values—and usually only between three and five core values—never change, unlike business strategies and tactics that change constantly to adapt to the global business environment. They also highlight an important point in their article: that "the role of core ideology is to guide and inspire, not differentiate. Two companies can have the same core values or purpose."[92]

Example: IBM

The history of IBM is one of both tremendous successes and a near permanently damaging stumble, but under the leadership of CEO Louis V. Gerstner Jr. beginning in the early 1990s, the company transformed itself successfully once again.

Approximately a decade ago, under the leadership of CEO Samuel J. Palmisano, IBM undertook a reexamination of its core values and crystallized the initiative in the tagline, "Some companies manage by rules. Some by hierarchies. IBM manages by its values."[93] While this is indeed a memorable and impressive company tagline, it is clear by even a cursory examination of IBM's public-facing statements about the process that underpinned the creation of this statement that it truly represents the heart and soul of the organization. In fact, here is what CEO Palmisano said at the time about the process that created the company's core values:

> In 2003, IBM undertook the first reexamination of its values in nearly 100 years. Through "Values-Jam," an unprecedented 72-hour discussion on IBM's global intranet, IBMers came together to define the essence of the company. The result? A set of core values, defined by IBMers for IBMers, that shape the way we lead, the way we decide, and the way we act.[94]

Generative Thinking

IBM's generative thinking approach to codifying its core values is an effective and creative mechanism to embed those values in the organization right from the start of the process. Although IBM changed its values, which seems to run counter to the notion that these values should be timeless and fixed, you can argue that making a change every hundred years is within the spirit of that rule. The three powerful, simple, and easy-to-remember values listed below reflect the very heart of IBM:

1. Dedication to every client's success

2. Innovation that matters, for our company and for the world

3. Trust and personal responsibility in all relationships[95]

Here is a final point about IBM's core-value creation process and its continuing work and commitment to the importance of promoting core values. Every two years, for the past decade, IBM has surveyed CEOs around the world to gauge the perspective of global leaders on emerging trends and issues. I personally participated in several of these surveys, and they were well done. One of the key emphasis areas in the 2012 report was the importance of organizational values. Here are the conclusions from the survey:

> Build values employees will live out. Allow the organization to collectively compose its core values. Thinking and behaving in ways consistent with the organization's values cannot be induced. Employees must truly believe in the purpose, mission, and values of the organization, and to develop a shared belief system, employees must help create it.[96]

Example: My Personal Company

Recently, I started my own management-consulting practice, Salvatore Fazzolari Advisors LLC. As I was contemplating the start-up of my practice, the first order of business was the codification of my core philosophy. My mission statement is, "To help clients win through insight, perspective, and generative thinking." I believe that the mission statement will clearly guide all engagements, because the purpose of the business will be to help clients win—that is, achieve success. Winning will be accomplished through three vital precocious characteristics: insight, perspective, and generative thinking.

After careful consideration, I settled on three core values. I believe that three is the optimum number, and after many years of working with them, I can clearly see why Collins and Porras provided the guideline of three to five. In fact, in their *Harvard Business Review* article, they make a strong and effective point about the number of values: "If you articulate more than five or six, chances are you are confusing your values with operating practices."[97]

Here are my company's three core values:

1. Integrity and trust in all engagements

2. Client service delivered with excellence and passion

3. Commitment to the advancement of the client

These three core values are easy to remember and capture the essence of what I believe in: integrity, winning, excellence, passion, commitment, and customer focus.

Example: Harsco

In early 2008, Harsco began its transformation journey by building the foundation of its core philosophy. The philosophy was codified during our "Good to Great" dialogue sessions, which are reviewed in chapter 8, "Distinctive Culture."

The mission statement that the executive leadership team codified fit the company well. Because of Harsco's global footprint and the way services and products were usually delivered at the customer site, the core mission statement was built around the key words of *teams, winning, integrity,* and *world.* Although many of these core beliefs already existed in the company, they had not been codified into a specific mission statement. That's just what the executive leadership team decided to do. Here is the statement we created:

To build *teams* that *win* with *integrity* anywhere in the *world*.

Teams means: customers, employees, shareholders, and suppliers.

Win means: value creation, value capture, value selling, be the best, and sustainable superior performance.

Integrity means: safety; ethical in thought, word and deed; disciplined thought, disciplined action, and disciplined people; transparency; personal accountability; and responsibility.

World means: customers, targeted markets, and envisioned future.

Subsequent to forming the core mission statement, we developed a tagline used in all of our external and internal presentations to augment the core purpose: "We Help Build the World."

In retrospect, I wish we had incorporated this tagline into the mission statement to improve clarity while maintaining the critical elements of winning, integrity, and teamwork across the globe. Here is what a revised mission statement could have looked like when merging the two elements: "To help build the world with teams that win with integrity."

Harsco's Core Values

Instead of highlighting a keyword in each core value, we underpinned each value with mechanisms that we either had developed, were in the process of developing, or planned to develop in the future. These mechanisms were intended to be embedded into the core values of the organization. The executive leadership team passionately believed that the company should be managed around the following four core values:

1. *Uncompromising integrity and ethical business practice.* The first core value was underpinned by what we called Harsco's integrity framework, which was made up of our well-defined and well-established code of conduct, safety policies and practices, internal control standards, security practices, and global management practices.

2. *People—the A-team.* The second core value was forward-looking and underpinned by what we called the human-capital framework. This is discussed in chapter 7, "People Excellence."

3. *Continuous improvement.* The third core value was underpinned by our Lean program and business-transformation initiative, which we were in the process of developing and implementing.

4. *Value-creation discipline.* The final core value was underpinned by our EVA framework and value-selling initiative, both of which were already well established in the company.

Exemplary Mission Statements

A mission statement or core purpose defines an organization; it represents the reason for the organization's existence. A mission statement should be relatively short and well-known, embraced and applied with passion by everyone in the organization. Here are eight mission statements I consider best-of-class:

> *Google*: "To organize the world's information and make it universally accessible and useful."[98]

> *eBay*: "To provide a global online marketplace where practically anyone can trade practically anything, enabling economic opportunity around the world."[99]

> *Southwest Airlines*: "To connect people to what's important in their lives through friendly, reliable, and low-cost air travel."[100]

Union Pacific: "The men and women of Union Pacific are dedicated to serve."[101]

Coca-Cola: "To refresh the world ... To inspire moments of optimism and happiness ... To create value and make a difference."[102]

Facebook: "To give people the power to share and make the world more open and connected."[103]

Hearst Corporation: "To inform, entertain and inspire."[104]

Singularity University: "To educate, inspire and empower leaders to apply exponential technologies to address humanity's grand challenges."[105]

Clearly, these organizations have worked hard to create powerful and effective mission statements. If your organization is in the process of developing a mission statement or reworking an existing mission statement, these examples should not only be inspirational but they can also function as a guide.

Menu of Possible Core Values

We have just examined phenomenal mission statements. In this section, I want to provide a multitude of core-value ideas that warrant consideration if your organization is in the process of developing or reworking existing values. However, before we examine these potential values, let's first review an excellent example of core values from the industrial company Danaher. This example will provide a good point of reference as your company embarks on its journey to define or redefine its core values. Here are the five core values of Danaher, as displayed on its website:[106]

1. The Best Team Wins
2. Customers Talk, We Listen

3. Continuous Improvement (Kaizen) Is Our Way of Life

4. Leading Edge Innovation Defines Our Future

5. We Compete for Shareholders

In formulating your core values, it is important to combine words like *integrity* with *honor* or with *trust*. Also, remember to follow the process used by IBM when establishing your core values. IBM's approach is generative because everyone in the organization is engaged in the process. Ultimately, all employees will need to embrace and live the core values every moment of their career, so it makes sense to get buy-in from the beginning. Choose from these key core values that are meaningful and strong. In no particular order:

» integrity	» entrepreneurial
» people	» leadership
» customer	» trust
» passion	» innovation
» accountability	» win
» courage	» safety
» teamwork	» personal responsibility
» creativity	» partnership
» respect	» collaboration
» loyalty	» giving back
» honesty	» long-term
» humility	» listen
» honor	» perseverance
» commitment	» candor
» continuous improvement	» have fun
» value creation	
» performance excellence	

Takeaways

In this chapter, we reviewed the elements of building a strong foundation: the core values and mission statement (core purpose). A core ideology was first brought to prominence by Jim Collins and Jerry Porras in *Built to Last*. The core mission must be clear and precise because it drives all actions of the organization. The core values are the beliefs of the company.

As the IBM CEO study pointed out, companies today are building a value system that employees live out. It is vital that employees in the organization believe and live every moment the values and mission of the enterprise. These values need to be properly embedded, so it is crucial for the enterprise to use an appropriate and effective mechanism to achieve this.

Numerous examples are provided of the core philosophy. IBM's approach to developing its core values is a paragon of excellence that can be emulated by others in establishing a core philosophy.

PART 3

The Serendipity of Chance, Good and Bad

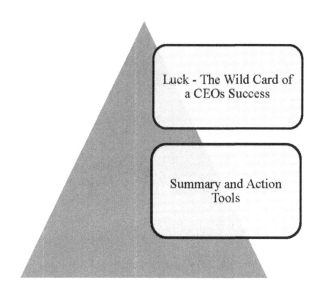

Luck - The Wild Card of a CEOs Success

Summary and Action Tools

Part 3 of this book provides insight and perspective on the wild card of a CEO's success: luck. This section also provides valuable tools and summaries for leaders to use in implementing the *CEO Lifelines* framework outlined in the book. A summary of each chapter follows:

» *Chapter 10: Luck—The Wild Card of a CEO's Success.* Luck impacts all leaders whether they admit it or not. The degree to which luck impacts a leader's life and success can be ameliorated by preparing for the worst and best of outcomes. Leaders who do this well most likely will be on the positive side of the luck spread.

» *Chapter 11: Summary and Action Tools.* This chapter includes summaries and a number of action-oriented tools, in checklist format, to help leaders plan for a positive future by implementing all the lifelines outlined in this book.

CHAPTER 10

Luck—The Wild Card of a CEO's Success

Ability is nothing without opportunity.
—Napoleon Bonaparte[107]

Never underestimate the power of luck. It touches the personal and professional life of us all, and it impacts which level of success (or even failure) is ultimately achieved by every enterprise. We live in a world of growing uncertainty and complexity, so it's important to be able to separate personal skill from luck and to give each an appropriate amount of credit.

At the same time, a leader by definition is not someone who typically even acknowledges luck in any way, and most would agree with the cliché about "making your own luck." I would not argue with this and fully embrace its message. However, we all know that somewhere in the story of every successful leader or enterprise is some small percentage of luck. That's why I call luck the wild card of every successful leader and enterprise; it's also the intangible part of success that my luck spread is designed to help leaders manage.

To put this discussion in terms of the central mountain-climbing metaphor for this book, the authors Mark F. Twight and James Martin in their book *Extreme Alpinism: Climbing Light, Fast, and High* highlight the importance of knowing the difference between luck and skill:

> Beware of accidentally succeeding on a route above your ability. Success tends to breed ambition. The next time, a route of similar difficulty or danger may deliver the hard lesson that a single success at a high level may present luck and not skill. Learn to recognize when you lucked out and when you met the challenge. Without this understanding, such a victory will feed contempt for easy routes on forgiving mountains. Contempt leads to a casual attitude, which results in carelessness and ultimate failure on a grand scale. Respect the routes you complete and those that turn you back. Respect for the mountains is a cornerstone for a long and fruitful career.[108]

Luck Spread

Managing luck spread requires three upfront steps by a leader. First, acknowledge that luck has some part, no matter how small, in your success. Second, take appropriate proactive actions and work hard at staying on the positive side of the luck spread. Third, commit to implementing the nine lifelines outlined in this book, which will increase the probability of keeping your career and the enterprise you lead away from the negative side of the luck spread.

The table included in this chapter is a graphic illustration of my luck-spread concept. It shows how the luck spread is the cumulative value of all the negative bad-luck events compared with the cumulative value of all the positive good-luck events. If the total value of the negative events exceeds the value of the positive events, then the result is a negative luck spread. Conversely, if the total value of the positive events exceeds the value of the negative events, then the result is a positive luck spread. If the spread between the negative luck spread and the positive luck is significant, then you have an unbalanced luck spread (which is what the illustration shows). Moreover, if this unbalanced luck spread is deep into the negative zone, the situation can have a catastrophic effect on an individual leader and on the company he or she leads.

An effective tool for measuring the luck spread is an analysis of all the positive and negative events that could have an impact on the enterprise. This analysis should be completed by using a scale concept. The hypothetical illustration shows that the scale is materially being weighed down by the heavy burden of high-impact negative events. This exercise should then be expanded by assigning a weight or point system to each letter. For example, a high-impact event could be ten points, a medium-impact event could be five points, and a low-impact event one point. This would provide a mathematical underpinning to the analysis.

Impact Codes: H (High), M (Moderate), and L (Low)

(+) Positive	Impact	(-) Negative	Impact
Commodities	H	European Sovereign Debt Crisis	H
Innovation	L	US Financial/Economic Crisis	H
Low Interest Rates	M	Foreign Exchange Rates	M
Acquisitions	M	Arab Spring	L
Asset Sales	L	Construction Markets Collapse	H
		Government Regulatory Assault	L
		Pricing Pressure in Key Markets	H
		Commodity Creep	M
		Pension Costs	M
		Oil Prices	L

Business leaders and enterprises both need to take management guru Peter Drucker's advice to heart that "the best way to predict the future is to create it"[109] and get control of their potential luck spread by implementing the nine leadership lifelines I've discussed in this book.

The rest of this chapter provides further explanation and examples of the luck spread concept and the implementation of its concepts into your life and career.

Thoughts on Luck

The late actress Shirley Temple Black once said about luck that it "needs no explanation."[110] But that's not entirely true, especially if you believe that you might arrange circumstances and events so that luck falls more in your favor. The author Nassim Nicholas Taleb skillfully stated in his book *The Black Swan* that what separates successful leaders from the unsuccessful is the great equalizer of luck.[111] Even the *Wall Street Journal* noted in a 2009 article on compensation that luck can sometimes impact the outcome. "What if the CEO was lucky enough to have been in the right place at the right time?" the article asks. "When it comes to a company's current performance, history matters, culture matters, markets matter, even weather can matter. How many chief executives have succeeded simply by maneuvering themselves into favorable situations and then hanging on while taking credit for all the success?"[112]

In the book *The Luck Factor*, Dr. Richard Wiseman explores the impact of luck in a wide span of personal, business, career, and scientific discovery situations. Wiseman provides a penetrating view of luck for his readers:

> Luck exerts a dramatic influence over our lives. A few seconds of bad fortune can unravel years of striving, while a moment of good luck can lead to success and happiness. Luck has the power to transform the improbable into the possible; to make the difference between life and death, reward and ruin, happiness and despair. ... The effects of good and bad luck are not confined to matters of life or death. They can also make the difference between financial reward and ruin.[113]

Jim Collins explores luck in his classic book *Great by Choice* and provides some compelling data to support his points. I thought Collins summed up luck particularly well when he wrote the following:

> We observed an asymmetry between good luck and bad. A single stroke of good fortune, no matter how big, cannot by itself make a great company. But a single stroke of extremely bad luck, or an extended sequence of bad-luck events that create a catastrophic outcome, can terminate the quest. There's only one truly definitive form of luck, and that's the luck that ends the game.[114]

Collins also makes an interesting point about how the role of luck is discounted in his marvelous book *How the Mighty Fall*: "Instead of acknowledging that luck and fortuitous events might have played a helpful role, people begin to presume that success is due entirely to the superior qualities of the enterprise and its leadership."[115] An example of an organization that clearly understands this point is the asset management firm of Harding Loevner, as indicated in this passage from its 2012 Annual Commentary report:

> We pursue relentlessly the elusive goal of perfection in the design and execution of our investment decision-making processes. For example, we must address the fact that human memory is poor ... *selectively* poor. When people experience favorable outcomes they tend, in hindsight, to attribute their results to skill and foresight. Objective observers, on the other hand, might describe the outcome as simply lucky! Among those who study human behavior, such "attribution" and "hindsight" biases are well understood.[116]

Clearly, the body of work on luck is compelling. The best way to illustrate the power of luck is to examine real-life examples. In the next section, we will review four actual cases of the luck spread—two positive and two negative.

Positive Luck-Spread Examples

The May 2013 issue of *Fortune* magazine provides a great example of how Corning took advantage of its positive luck spread to chart a successful future course:

> In the 1970s Corning began developing glass tubes that could carry information in pulses of light: fiber optics. As the Internet rose, so did Corning's stock. But then the dotcom bubble burst, and the company found itself in need of another hit. Serendipitously, Steve Jobs called. He wanted a thin and very strong glass for Apple's new smartphone. And he wanted it in production in six months. Corning dusted off and modified an old project it had first pitched to the auto industry 50 years earlier, modified it, and ended up with Gorilla Glass, a line that nearly all glass touch-screens are made of today. Sales have doubled every year since it was first introduced in 2008.[117]

Just imagine being the CEO of Corning and receiving a call from Steve Jobs at Apple. And imagine being fortunate enough to have a product on the shelf that was developed fifty years earlier and provided the basic technology.

In the book *Playing to Win: How Strategy Really Works*, authors A. G. Lafley and Roger L. Martin provide another excellent example of luck, in this case how it played a part in the success of Procter & Gamble:

> Some things, however, happen by way of serendipity, and the acquisition of Max Factor is a perfect case in point. Max Factor was acquired to make the P&G cosmetics business more global. That really never panned out. Max Factor did sufficiently poorly in North America so that is was discontinued there. Nor did it provide much of a cosmetics platform outside North America. So, the acquisition would likely be called out, the

cosmetics business came along with two businesses—a small fine-fragrances portfolio and a tiny, super-high-end Japanese skin-care business called SK-II. That fragrance portfolio became the seed of a multi-billion-dollar, world leading fine-fragrances business. SK-II has expanded into international markets and has crossed the billion-dollar mark in global sales, with extremely attractive profitability. In this case, serendipity smiled on P&G.[118]

My Own Positive Luck Spread

While it's true that I encountered a negative luck spread while serving as CEO of Harsco, my own life story is a great example of a positive luck spread. It's a story that began in the small Italian town in Mammola, Calabria, where I was born and, through a series of unlikely events, brought me to the pinnacle of business success in the United States. If you want to read the entire story of my positive personal-life luck spread, see appendix 2, "The Power of Luck—My Journey."

Negative Luck-Spread Examples

The stories of Corning and P&G are clear positive luck-spread examples, but how is a negative luck-spread manifested? While it is easy to find examples in other organizations, perhaps my own negative luck-spread experiences at Harsco are the most instructive. We will also review a second example involving an extraordinary mountaineer.

My story can be told by comparing two sets of three-year periods and explaining what happened between those periods. During the period of 2006 through 2008, Harsco posted record positive results. However, in the period between the years 2009 and 2011, Harsco posted much different results, particularly during the years 2010 and 2011.

I served as president for the first two of those six years and was

CEO for the remaining four years, so what happened? In four simple words: extreme global economic shocks! The luck spread was immensely negative. The first shock was the US financial and economic crisis in late 2008, followed by the European sovereign debt crisis. These two events had a profound and material negative impact on Harsco's two largest service and equipment businesses, which relied on the global construction and steel markets. The European business was particularly impacted due to Harsco's historically heavy concentration in that market.

As CEO, I certainly felt the impact of what Collins calls in *Great by Choice* "an extended sequence of bad-luck events [that] create a catastrophic outcome." My personal experience was certainly that!

In an edition of the book *The Climb: Tragic Ambitions on Everest* by Anatoli Boukreev and G. Weston DeWalt that was published after Boukreev's death, DeWalt added an "In Memory" section that illustrates the way in which tremendous skill is no shield against bad luck. He describes an incident in May 1996 in which Boukreev, in an effort some described as suicidal, went out into a ferocious blizzard to rescue three stranded climbers. His extraordinary actions saved the climbers' lives and earned him the American Alpine Club's most prestigious award. Only three weeks after winning that award, Boukreev was killed (Christmas Day 1997) in an avalanche that also took the life of a fellow climber but spared a third.[119] Even with all of Boukreev's precocious characteristics, indispensable experiences, and proactive actions, the luck spread on that day was extremely negative. Sadly, his quest ended and the world lost a talented and courageous mountaineer.

The important takeaway from all of these examples is that luck is indeed a factor and, as the *Wall Street Journal* article points out, markets matter, geography matters, and history matters. Unremittingly negative luck events can ultimately cause the luck spread to be significantly negative, which in turn can have dire consequences.

What Conclusions Can Be Drawn?

First, you can conclude that luck is real! Don't try to ignore it or pretend that it doesn't exist. Once you understand this fact, you can take positive action to improve your chances and your particular situation. Second, you must conclude that it is critical to stay on the positive side of the luck spread, and that a deep understanding of the variables that can impact your luck spread is essential.

The good news in all of this is that you can proactively pull the right levers to help improve and rebalance the luck spread and possibly push it to the positive. The first and most important step in this journey is accomplished by building and implementing the nine essential lifelines I describe in this book. Finally, it is important to recognize that sometimes no matter what you do, a single stroke of bad luck or a series of bad-luck events can end the journey.

The Luck Factor and the Nine Lifelines

The research done by Dr. Richard Wiseman in his book *The Luck Factor* provides a bridge to the power of luck and helps underpin my contention that implementing the nine lifelines outlined in this book increases your probability of positive luck spread. Wiseman distilled his research down to four principles of luck. He breaks down these four principles into several subprinciples so that there are twelve subprinciples in all. Wiseman says the four principles of luck include an admonition to maximize your chance opportunities, listen to your luck hunches, expect good fortune, and turn your bad luck into good.[120] Let's look at each of these in more detail along with their subprinciples.

1. Maximize Your Chance Opportunities

The author underpins this principle with three subprinciples that capture its essence and include the following:

» Lucky people build and maintain a strong "network of luck."

» Lucky people have a relaxed attitude toward life (low level of anxiety).

» Lucky people are open to new experiences in their lives.

I believe that this first principle and related subprinciples are consistent with my point that you can increase your probability of success and tip the balance of the luck spread to positive by building and implementing all nine leadership lifelines. A similar insightful point was also made centuries ago by President Thomas Jefferson when he said, "I'm a great believer in luck, and I find the harder I work the more I have of it."[121]

2. Listen to Your Luck Hunches

The author underpins this principle with two subprinciples:

» Lucky people listen to their gut feelings and hunches.

» Lucky people take steps to boost their intuition.

This second principle and related subprinciples are consistent with chapter 1, "Precocious Characteristics."

3. Expect Good Fortune

Wiseman underpins this principle with three subprinciples that again support the main themes in this book about the importance of luck. They are:

» Lucky people expect their good luck to continue in the future.

» Lucky people attempt to achieve their goals, even if their chances of success seem slim, and persevere in the face of failure.

» Lucky people expect their interactions with others to be lucky and successful.

This principle is consistent with my recommendation to build as many lifelines as possible. By vigorously implementing the nine leadership lifelines, you may be able to tip the luck spread back to the positive.

4. Turn Your Bad Luck into Good

The author underpins this principle with four subprinciples. They are:

- » Lucky people see the positive side of their bad luck.
- » Lucky people are convinced that any ill fortune in their life will, in the long run, work out for the best.
- » Lucky people do not dwell on their ill fortune.
- » Lucky people take constructive steps to prevent more bad luck in the future.

Again, this principle and its related subprinciples are consistent with building lifelines as discussed throughout this book.

Takeaways

We have to recognize that luck, both positive and negative, is a factor and in some cases can be a major factor in our careers and in the destiny of an enterprise. Good luck can be an enabler and positively advance the cause of a leader and the organization he or she leads. Conversely, a series of bad-luck events can turn the luck spread significantly negative, which can ultimately destroy a leader's career and impair an enterprise. It is crucial to avoid the "luck that ends the game." This can be mitigated by vigorously implementing the nine lifelines outlined in this book.

CHAPTER 11

Summary and Action Tools

Great thoughts speak only to the thoughtful mind,
but great actions speak to all mankind.
—*Theodore Roosevelt*[122]

In the previous ten chapters, we reviewed the nine lifelines and the power of the luck spread. This chapter includes summaries and a number of action-oriented diagnostic tools derived from this work. All the salient points from *CEO Lifelines* are summarized and organized into a checklist format. Checklists are vital, and they are effectively used in mountaineering and in many industries—particularly in financial services, innovation, aviation, medical, and environmental practices, but in just about every other business sector as well.

Just as checklists are helpful to mountaineers in preparing for their climb, they can also be helpful to leaders to implement and assess the nine lifelines and to better understand the luck spread. Checklists are also included in this chapter for self-created enterprise lifelines, mechanisms, risk assessment, board responsibilities, and for the ten most important rules for CEOs to live by. Finally, there's a comprehensive checklist of all recommended readings.

Let's begin with an overview of the nine lifelines identified in this book.

Lifeline 1: Precocious Characteristics

Leaders must possess thirty critical characteristics to succeed as leaders and move their organization forward. Some are innate and others must be developed, but leadership strength and suitability is defined by these characteristics. In addition, leaders must undertake an inventory and make an honest assessment of these critical intangible qualities. The following checklist should be used to determine how many of these precocious characteristics you possess. Each characteristic must then be assessed as to its depth and quality. A plan for improvement must also be developed. Make sure that you enlist an independent and objective party to assist with the exercise. Here is the list of the thirty precocious characteristics:

» integrity
» instincts
» perspective
» discipline
» wisdom
» willingness to apologize
» loyalty
» navigational skills
» optimism and passion
» good execution
» humility
» communication skills
» ability to be proactive
» transparency
» inquisitiveness
» truthfulness
» courage
» cost mind-set
» ability to build an enduring enterprise
» generative thinking
» continuous self-improvement
» equanimity
» negotiating skills
» gratefulness
» giving nature
» team-building talents
» accountability
» perseverance
» survival instincts
» learning, teaching, and coaching ability

Lifeline 2: Indispensable Experiences

In order to ascend to the summit, leaders must have an ability to learn through indispensable experiences. These experiences will define a leader. CEOs must be better than most at gathering up the right collection of experiences and skills through proactive actions. Activities that should be considered when thinking about the cumulative right experiences include those that have the following characteristics:

» instructive and insightful

» developmental and character-building

» formative and impactful

» cultural and technical

A talent-management and leadership-development process must ensure that the right experiences are provided to future CEOs, as well as newly appointed CEOs. The talent-management and leadership-development process should provide the following:

» robust succession-planning process

» challenging stretch assignments, including significant overseas appointments

» experience managing a large business and possibly the entire company as COO or president

» a mentor (assigned naturally and informally)

» an immersion-experience, high-quality training program

» total support from the board and senior leadership team

» an opportunity to develop outside connections, including joining a board of another company

Lifeline 3: Proactive Actions

Leaders need a fearless and proactive approach to the job. CEOs and leaders can follow the recipe for success through proactive actions. The recipe includes the following ingredients:

» Possess a proactive mind-set.

» Develop a road map of proactive actions, with key inputs including inventory and assessment of lifelines as well as individual precocious characteristics.

» Build an appropriate number of lifelines by networking and reaching out to key individuals and organizations.

» Cultivate indispensable experiences through proactive action.

» Focus on learning and continuous self-improvement.

» Protect one's reputation.

» Take certain basic proactive actions when assuming a new leadership position.

» Implement the ten critical proactive actions once appointed as a leader.

» Implement certain specific proactive actions after one year in a leadership position.

The *basic, critical,* and *specific* proactive actions include the following and are identified as (B), (C), and (S):

» Sign an appropriate agreement. (B)

» Appoint an A-player as chief human-resource officer. (B)

» Sharpen skills through learning and gain perspective. (B)

» Review all projects and strategies. (C)

» Focus on the customer and meet with investors. (C)

» Develop a strategic road map, envisioned future, and key performance metrics. (C)

» Establish the CEO relationship and understand the role of the board. (C)

» Pursue change with patience, wisdom, and a high level of skepticism. (C)

» Employ actions and antidotes to deal with CEO surprises. (C)

» Make safety a top priority and a core value. (C)

» Determine where true economic value is being created. (C)

» Develop a robust sales cadence, backlog, and forecasting system. (C)

» Bring the global leadership team together. (C)

» Seek appointment to outside board. (S)

» Conduct a 360 review. (S)

» Seek constructive feedback on performance from key board members. (S)

Lifeline 4: Business Model

The most complex task of leadership is discovering and implementing an innovative business model. There are two key elements to consider:

» recipe or unique set of activities

» organizational structure

There are essentially three broad organizational structures to choose from:

» *centralized or fully integrated model*, the characteristics of which include a homogeneous business; standardized and integrated information technology platform (one ERP); strong organizational skills; and standard global processes

» *decentralized model*, the characteristics of which include strong entrepreneurial culture; effective enterprise controls; consistent high performance; multiple business platforms (nonhomogeneous); and a majority of business not exposed to highly cyclical markets

» *hybrid or matrix model*, the characteristics of which include strong and talented functional leaders; high level of trust and teamwork in the organization; company operates as an entrepreneurial and proactive management company; standard processes; either multiple business platforms (nonhomogeneous) or single platform (homogeneous); and exceptional global capabilities like shared services, integrated supply chain, and Lean

Characteristics of an effective and innovative business model include the following, and they should be properly assessed to determine how your organization compares with the best:

» high gross margins

» recurring, predictable revenue streams

» strong operating margins

» high return on invested capital

» prodigious operating and free cash flows

» minimal capital expenditures

» efficient redeployment of capital

Roper is a paragon of excellence. The company's recipe includes the following elements, which you may want to check off for your company as well:

» cash return discipline that delivers compelling free cash flow

» niche-market leadership positions through a diverse set of businesses

» focus on proprietary and differentiated solutions that generate high gross margins

» exceptional operating managers who are accountable

» a nimble governance system

» asset-light businesses, minimal capital expenditures, and efficient working capital

» effective and efficient redeployment of free cash flow to drive growth

» strong growth prospects for acquisitions

Lifeline 5: Learning Entity

An enterprise must implement an appropriate number of mechanisms in order to ensure that it learns valuable and actionable lessons from both success and failure. Effective mechanisms include the following:

» key-seats executive retreat
» internal university
» postevent debrief
» learning committee
» joint ventures and strategic alliances

The focus, however, needs to be on lessons learned, both positive and negative. The following are the thirty most important lessons I've learned as a CEO, both inside and outside the company. These lessons are segmented as personal characteristics (1–6), people excellence (7–10), transformation and reinvention (11–20), uncertainty and turbulence (21–22), execution and focus (23–25), and board-related matters (26–30):

1. Don't discount your instinct—go with it.
2. Don't assume that everyone will be like you.
3. Remember, it's not your job to make friends.
4. Be proactive in protecting your position and reputation.
5. Treat all people equally and with respect.
6. Allow for a period of inner reflection and growth.
7. Get an A-player for the chief human-resources officer.
8. Promote from within, and limit senior-management-level outside hires.
9. Establish the appropriate mechanisms to embed and assess people characteristics.
10. Create a winning culture.

11. Manage change well—too many changes are highly disruptive and stressful.

12. Create an effective communication plan.

13. Effectively define, manage, and communicate transformational change.

14. Think differently and adapt to change.

15. Carefully consider investments in high-capital-expenditure businesses.

16. Invest and grow "niche" businesses.

17. Evaluate the business portfolio early in your tenure.

18. Be audacious when undertaking a major restructuring action.

19. Rebuild your balance sheet.

20. Unleash the power of scalability.

21. Deal decisively with global shocks and economic turbulence.

22. Analyze possible scenarios and prepare for the worst.

23. Integrate acquisitions immediately.

24. Do not focus primarily on the competition.

25. Do not rely on a single metric.

26. Don't make too many board changes.

27. Use an effective internal sourcing process to recruit board members.

28. Create a solid CEO succession-planning process.

29. Decide whether to combine or separate the roles of chairman and CEO.

30. Join at least one board.

Lifeline 6: Exceptional Capabilities

Strong operational capabilities and their consistent execution increase the potential for value creation and sustainable, competitive advantage. There are twenty must-have exceptional capabilities. In addition, an enterprise must undertake a vigorous lifelines inventory and assessment of its capabilities. The ultimate goal of every leader must be to create an elite enterprise. An elite enterprise is one that has the following characteristics:

> » adaptable and proactive
>
> » global in reach and mind-set
>
> » driven by an innovative and entrepreneurial business model
>
> » generates prodigious free cash flow and strong operating results
>
> » founded on a clear mission statement and strong core values
>
> » home to an exceptional management team

An important step in creating such an enterprise is following the twenty exceptional capabilities, which are segmented into three philosophical strategies of *optimization, innovation,* and *globalization.* These three elements are identified as (O), (I), and (G) in the following list:

> » Enhance the cash conversion cycle. (O)
>
> » Improve capital efficiency. (O)
>
> » Use an integrated global supply chain. (O)
>
> » Set up global shared services. (O)
>
> » Employ Lean and Six-Sigma. (O)
>
> » Execute a product-management strategy. (O)
>
> » Take advantage of pricing power and value selling. (O)
>
> » Implement a variable cost model. (O)
>
> » Review the global legal and tax structure. (O)
>
> » Develop exceptional project-management skills. (O)

» Focus on brand development. (I)

» Invest in science and innovation. (I)

» Design an effective talent-management system. (I)

» Monitor sales cadence, backlog, and forecasting. (I)

» Do a real-time scan of the environment. (I)

» View information technology as a strategic asset. (I)

» Seek out joint ventures and strategic alliances. (I, G)

» Target strategic acquisitions. (I, G)

» Maintain disciplined growth. (G)

» Identify frontier markets. (G)

Lifeline 7: People Excellence

Building an exceptional team is vital to the success of a leader and the enterprise, but it is nearly impossible to do without a powerful internal talent-management and leadership-development process. Selecting, developing, and retaining the right team is the most important responsibility of a CEO. There are nine critical personal and team characteristics plus three more that should be considered when looking for the right person. They include the following:

» integrity and ethics

» a willingness to be a team player

» an ability to consistently deliver high results

» a good fit with core values

» an ability to self-manage with minimal guidance

» an understanding and acceptance of responsibilities

» consistency and follow-through in what he or she says and does

» acceptance of responsibility and accountability for actions, including giving appropriate credit to others for success

» passion for and pride in the company's culture

The following are additional personal characteristics that warrant consideration:

» effective communication skills

» ability to think critically

» loyalty

An alternative and recommended approach to assessing the key-seats leadership team of the enterprise is to use the thirty characteristics in chapter 1, "Precocious Characteristics." In building an A-team, there are some critical actions that need to be taken, including the following:

» Define the global leadership team, which is the largest group. It usually includes all the top managers, officers, and executives of the enterprise.

» Define the key-seats leadership team, which is the second largest group. It usually includes all the key direct reports to the CEO and direct reports one level down.

» Define the executive leadership team, which is the smallest and most senior group and usually includes all the key direct reports to the CEO.

» Develop talent internally through a robust and innovative practice.

» Promote from within, avoiding outside hires for senior management positions.

Lifeline 8: Distinctive Culture

Building and sustaining a high-functioning and harmonious culture is essential if an organization is going to endure. A company with a dysfunctional or disharmonious culture will most likely not perform as well over a long horizon. Good leaders understand the importance of a strong, unified culture where everyone is aligned, disciplined, and focused on five core elements. Here are the five elements that must be in place for a distinctive and healthy culture:

» core mission and underpinning values

» character of the right people

» the right business model

» leader excellence

» effective mechanisms

Roper and RPM are two examples of a distinctive and effective culture. This is particularly important for successful business transformations.

Lifeline 9: Core Philosophy

A core philosophy is built around an enterprise's mission statement and core values and is the true heart and soul of any organization. Without this core philosophy firmly in place, building a successful and long-lasting enterprise is impossible. Remember that the role of the core philosophy is to guide and inspire, not differentiate an organization. Thus, two companies can have similar or identical values or purpose. The following must be understood in developing a core philosophy:

» The core philosophy has two parts: a core mission (or purpose) and core values.

» A mission statement or core purpose is the organization's most fundamental reason for being. It must be clearly understood and embraced by everyone in the organization.

» Core values are a handful of guiding principles by which a company navigates. They must also be clearly understood and embraced by everyone. There should be no more than three to five core values.

» The vision framework of an enterprise is made up of both the core philosophy and envisioned future.

A mission statement must be clear, and an organization must relentlessly adhere to it. There are many excellent examples of strong mission statements that can be found by searching the websites of top companies. Here are a few exceptional examples, particularly the first three, that will be helpful in formulating your organization's mission statement:

» Google: "To organize the world's information and make it universally accessible and useful."

» eBay: "To provide a global online marketplace where practically anyone can trade practically anything, enabling economic opportunity around the world."

» Southwest Airlines: "To connect people to what's important in their lives through friendly, reliable, and low-cost air travel."

» Union Pacific: "The men and women of Union Pacific are dedicated to serve."

» Coca-Cola: "To refresh the world … To inspire moments of optimism and happiness … To create value and make a difference."

» Facebook: "To give people the power to share and make the world more open and connected."

» Hearst Corporation: "To inform, entertain and inspire."

» Singularity University: "To educate, inspire and empower leaders to apply exponential technologies to address humanity's grand challenges."

» My new company: "To help clients win through insight, perspective, and generative thinking."

» Harsco: "To build teams that win with integrity anywhere in the world."

Just like the mission statement, the core values of an organization need to be clear and fully embraced by everyone in the organization. There are numerous examples of strong core values that can be found by searching the websites of strong companies. Here are some examples of core values that will be helpful in formulating your value system:

» Dedication to every client's success. (IBM)

» Innovation that matters, for our company and for the world. (IBM)

» Trust and personal responsibility in all relationships. (IBM)

» The best teams win. (Danaher)

» Customers talk, we listen. (Danaher)

» Continuous improvement (Kaizen) is our way of life. (Danaher)

» Leading-edge innovation defines our future. (Danaher)

» We compete for shareholders. (Danaher)

» Uncompromising integrity and ethical business practice. (Harsco)

» People—the "A-Team." (Harsco)

» Continuous improvement. (Harsco)

» Value creation discipline. (Harsco)

» Integrity and trust in all engagements. (my company)

» Client service delivered with excellence and passion. (my company)

» Commitment to the advancement of the client. (my company)

In formulating your core values, it is important to remember the process used by IBM, where everyone in the organization was invited to participate in establishing the core values. Here is a list of key core value words that are meaningful and strong that will be helpful in formulating your core values:

» integrity
» people
» customer
» passion
» accountability
» courage
» teamwork
» creativity
» respect
» loyalty
» honesty
» humility
» honor
» commitment

» continuous improvement
» value creation
» performance excellence
» entrepreneurial
» leadership
» trust
» innovation
» win
» safety
» personal responsibility
» partnership

» collaboration
» giving back
» long-term
» listen
» perseverance
» candor
» have fun

Self-Created Enterprise Lifelines

Visionary leaders build lifelines during good times and over a long horizon (decades) to prepare for as yet unforeseen but inevitable global shocks. Building an abundant number of lifelines is vital to the long-term health and viability of an enterprise. Here is a list of crucial lifelines that leaders need to build in order to survive and possibly even thrive during major global shocks:

» Build a strong balance sheet and accumulate ample cash reserves.

» Reduce debt to very manageable levels.

» Invest in people and field an A-team.

» Invest in vigorous training and leadership development.

» Invest in innovation, science, and product development.

» Invest in continuous improvement skills using Lean or Six-Sigma.

» Invest in improving processes and strengthening exceptional capabilities.

» Develop an innovative business model.

» Minimize investment in fixed assets and physical locations.

» Reduce concentration in geography, customers, and cyclical markets.

» Implement a variable cost structure.

» Build a strong integrated supply chain.

» Invest in niche businesses that have minimal competition and are not subject to precipitous declines during economic turbulence.

» Build a learning entity.

» Implement mechanisms that are effective and promote a strong, unified culture.

Mechanisms

It is imperative that organizations have in place numerous mechanisms that are designed to improve the organization, provide early warning signs, and help keep the organization on the right path to excellence. Some examples of critical mechanisms that every organization should have in place include:

» inventory and assessment of lifelines

» postevent reviews and debriefs

» internal university

» disciplined and consistent growth metric, such as 20 Mile March

» over 90 percent of key seats filled with the right people

» talent-management and leadership-development framework that includes succession planning

» vision framework

» CEO communication tool kit: weekly business reviews, quarterly business reviews, blog to key seats, town halls, coffee with CEO

» core philosophy "tell a story" slide

» key performance metrics like EVA, ROIC, ROE, CROIC, and free cash flow growth

» monthly CEO report to board on strategic road-map execution

» periodic robust dialogue sessions to review ongoing projects and strategies

» global leadership team executive retreat

» key-seats leadership team

» executive leadership team

Risk Assessment

Risk assessment is one of the most important responsibilities of a CEO and the board of directors. It can work well with an understanding of the business model. The two need to be considered simultaneously. Some of the identified risks overlap with others. For example, reputation risk can be adversely affected by product recall, litigation, compliance violations, and others. Here are some of the key risk focus areas:

- » end-market concentration
- » customer concentration
- » geographic concentration
- » succession planning
- » large fixed-cost base
- » business model
- » significant capital expenditures
- » business cyclicality
- » declining gross and operating margins
- » preparing enterprise for the next global shock
- » supply-chain disruptions
- » too-large bets
- » too many changes
- » too many recruits from outside the company
- » currencies exposure
- » commodities exposure
- » number of key seats filled with the right people
- » geopolitical events
- » macroeconomic risk
- » major global shocks
- » reputation risk
- » execution risk
- » commodity trap
- » investment in people
- » innovation risk
- » regulatory assault
- » code-of-conduct violations
- » data-security risk
- » access to capital markets
- » litigation
- » product recall
- » compliance
- » financial-statements restatement
- » interest rates
- » international expansion
- » growth faster than the ability to fill key seats with the right people

Board of Directors: Key Responsibilities (Independent Directors)

The purpose of the board of directors is to serve and represent the owners. There are a multitude of responsibilities associated with board membership but none is more important than being accountable and responsible for choosing the CEO (including succession planning), managing risk, and overseeing the strategic plan of the enterprise. Here is a list of all the vital duties of the board:

» is accountable and responsible for the CEO

» ensures that there is a healthy corporate culture underpinned by high ethical standards

» ensures that there are robust processes for succession planning, talent management, and leadership development

» oversees enterprise risk

» oversees strategic planning, road map, and envisioned future

» oversees executive compensation

» establishes a strong compliance and corporate-governance framework

» ensures that critical decisions are based on unassailable facts and guards against attribution and opinion

» provides appropriate lifelines to new CEO

» ensures that appropriate enterprise-wide lifelines are built

» plans for a crisis

» works closely with management to establish an entrepreneurial culture

» works with CEO and provides sage advice in dealing with global shocks and navigating turbulence

» closely monitors the reputation risk of the enterprise and its leader

» consistently manifests sound judgment, wisdom, and perspective

» establishes proper key performance metrics for CEO

» requires CEO to obtain an outside board seat and assists in the effort

» rigorously assesses board performance and individual board members' continuous improvement

» oversees transformational and reinvention initiatives

» possesses substantial knowledge of the business and its key business-unit leaders

» understands that the board is not involved in managing the company

» is respectful of the CEO and the management team

» maintains and manifests an independent mind-set

» monitors investor relations closely

» establishes strong board culture

» takes the lead whenever a proposed transaction creates a possible conflict between shareholders and management

» closely monitors behavioral risk of executives

Ten Rules for CEOs and Leaders to Live By

I would like to summarize what I believe to be the ten rules by which all CEOs and leaders need to live. These are all covered either explicitly or implicitly in this book. Also, these rules assume that the leader is intensely focused on concurrently implementing all nine lifelines outlined in this book. How many of these rules are you following?

» Walk the talk and set the tone for the organization by manifesting integrity in every action, every word, and every deed.

» Go with your instinct, your sixth sense; it will never fail you.

» Learn to listen—there's so much to learn from others.

» Learn to stop doing, which can be more important than a to-do list.

» Manage in good times as you would in bad times.

» Prepare daily for your ascent to the summit with discipline.

» Engage everyone in the organization in robust dialogue and validate anecdotal comments and attribution with unimpeachable facts whenever possible.

» Consistently display a proactive mind-set.

» Be humble and maintain an unwavering faith that you will prevail no matter what the circumstances.

» Manifest passion, commitment, optimism, and wisdom in all actions and decisions.

Recommended Readings

There are many books and other readings referenced throughout *CEO Lifelines* that would be of benefit to leaders. Check off these important books as you read them:

» *Steve Jobs* by Walter Isaacson

» *Good to Great* by Jim Collins

» *Great by Choice* by Jim Collins and Morton Hansen

» *Built to Last* by Jim Collins and Jerry I. Porras

» *How the Mighty Fall* by Jim Collins

» *Strategic Capitalism: The New Economic Strategy for Winning the Capitalist Cold War* by Dr. Richard A. D'Aveni

» *Beating the Commodity Trap* by Dr. Richard A. D'Aveni

» *Who Says Elephants Can't Dance?* by Louis V. Gerstner Jr.

» *Understanding Michael Porter* by Joan Magretta

» *Jack: Straight from the Gut* by Jack Welch, with John A. Byrne

» *Playing to Win: How Strategy Really Works* by A. G. Lafley and Roger L. Martin

» *Effective Apology: Mending Fences, Building Bridges, and Restoring Trust* by John Kador

» *Extreme Alpinism: Climbing Light, Fast, and High* by Mark F. Twight and James Martin

» *Alpine Climbing: Techniques to Take You Higher* by Mark Houston and Kathy Cosley

» *The Black Swan: The Impact of the Highly Improbable* by Nassim Nicholas Taleb

» *The Luck Factor* by Dr. Richard Wiseman

» *Mountaineering: The Freedom of the Hills* edited by Ronald C. Eng

» *The Climb: Tragic Ambitions on Everest* by Anatoli Boukreev and G. Weston DeWalt

» *Every Nation for Itself* by Dr. Ian Bremmer

» *Reinvent: A Leader's Playbook for Serial Success* by Fred Hassan

» *College (Un)Bound* by Jeffrey J. Selingo

My most important readings previously mentioned in this book are these three published by *Harvard Business Review:*

» "Seven Surprises for New CEOs" by Michael E. Porter, Jay W. Lorsch, and Nitin Nohria

» "Building Your Company's Vision" by Jim Collins and Jerry I. Porras

» "What is Strategy?" by Michael E. Porter

FINAL REMARKS

I have spent my entire business career learning, studying, observing, and listening. This curiosity culminated in the writing of this book. Based on the multitude of business books I have read throughout my career, there's a particular gap that needs to be filled. To my knowledge, there is no one book that fully brings together in one place—in the form of a guidebook and checklists—all the important lifelines that I believe are necessary for a leader and an enterprise to be successful. My hope is that newly appointed leaders, as well as all aspiring leaders, will use this lifeline as a playbook and road map as they prepare every day for their climb to the summit.

As explained throughout the book, CEOs and other leaders at the top of the organization are a special breed. While they do share lower-level leadership characteristics, one indisputable fact sets them far apart from everyone else in the enterprise: no matter what happens in the organization, the ultimate responsibility always resides with them. By embracing and implementing the nine lifelines while at the same time understanding the power of the luck spread, I believe leaders can improve their chances of success and that of the enterprise they lead. In the two appendices that follow, I'll share personal stories about the ways I've found the luck spread to be true.

» **Appendix 1: Climb the Summit—Harsco's Journey.** This part of the book covers my experiences in leading Harsco's transformation journey, titled "Climb the Summit," while simultaneously dealing with the worst economic storm and turbulence in the modern history of the company. The purpose of including this journey is to provide readers with an additional perspective and more insight on the challenges and accomplishments of the team.

» **Appendix 2: The Power of Luck—My Journey.** This part of the book covers my positive luck-spread experiences. My positive luck events began when I was born in a small town called Mammola in the Italian province of Calabria. The purpose of including these events is to show the reader that everyone in life needs some positive luck as they ascend to the summit.

APPENDIX 1

Climb the Summit— Harsco's Journey

Once we accept our limits, we go beyond them.
—Albert Einstein[123]

As has been demonstrated throughout the book, the parallels between mountaineering and business are almost endless. That is why at Harsco I chose "Climb the Summit" as the theme for our transformation and reinvention journey. Before we examine Harsco's journey in more detail, let's review another insightful metaphor from mountaineering. The preface to the eighth edition of *Mountaineering: The Freedom of the Hills* states:

> Climbing requires continual awareness of the situation and environment at hand. Varying conditions, routes, and individual abilities all mean that the techniques used and decisions made must be based on the particular circumstances. To any situation, the individual climber and climbing team must apply their knowledge, skills, and experiences and then make their own judgments.[124]

"Climb the Summit" Journey

Harsco's "Climb the Summit" journey began with my appointment as CEO by the board in August 2007; I formally assumed the title on January 1, 2008. I was officially CEO for fifty months, and my tenure was extremely challenging. My new role commenced just before the financial and economic collapse. What timing on my part!

As explained earlier in the book, the US financial and economic crisis and later the European sovereign debt crisis significantly impacted Harsco. These two severe global economic shocks had a profound negative impact on our two largest businesses that operated in the cyclical construction and steel markets. The construction markets were hit particularly hard, with sales and pricing dropping precipitously. Exacerbating the situation were two other factors: first, the company had a significant overall historical commercial concentration in Europe (well over 50 percent of revenues), and second, due to the decentralized business model (over 450 locations in about fifty-two countries), the fixed-cost structure was difficult to sustain with declining revenues and pricing.

As I explained in chapter 4, "Business Model," the trade-off with a decentralized business model is usually a higher fixed-cost structure because of the people, locations, and equipment that are needed to support the business location. Thus, during a severe economic downturn (in our case, the worst in the modern history of the company), this type of structure is often difficult to sustain. One can say that we faced the so-called perfect storm. The company flew right into the eye of the storm and its colossal disturbance. Lamentably, major lifelines were in short supply because of the severity of the economic meltdown in our key end-markets.

The simplest way to illustrate the dramatic negative impact of the perfect economic storm on Harsco is to examine the revenues of the company. In 2008, revenues peaked at $4 billion; one year later, they plunged 25 percent to $3 billion. Needless to say, the bottom line is severely impacted when revenues drop so precipitously.

The State of the Company before the Storm

Before we examine the perfect storm in more detail, it is important to understand the company's operations as well as the state of the enterprise. At the beginning of 2008, Harsco was a multinational company with revenues of approximately $3 billion. Those revenues were approximately 83 percent services and 17 percent products. The majority of the company's revenues (70 percent) were generated outside the United States.

Just like many multinational companies during the period leading up to late 2007, the record performance of Harsco benefited from strong tailwinds, especially the global economic bubble and a weak US dollar. Both of these tailwinds were naturally unsustainable, particularly for multinational companies that operated in market sectors like construction and steel. These tailwinds ultimately turned into headwinds. With this background, the company, in my view, needed to urgently transform itself in order to meet what I saw (by instinct) as emerging global challenges. Dark clouds were already starting to form in late 2007 and early 2008, as I discussed in chapter 8, "Distinctive Culture."

Transformation Strategy

As part of the transformation and reinvention strategy, we reorganized the company under four segments: Harsco Metals & Minerals, Harsco Infrastructure, Harsco Rail, and Harsco Industrial. A brief description of each refocused segment follows.

» *Harsco Metals & Minerals* was the world's largest provider of onsite, outsourced services to the global metals industries, principally the steel market. This is mostly a services business with some products developed by the minerals side of the company. Environmentally-led, mineral-based products for a range of commercial and industrial uses along with recycling solutions for global resources recovery best defines this business.

» *Harsco Infrastructure* was a global leader in highly engineered rental scaffolding, shoring, concrete-forming, and other access-related services. This was entirely a services business. A solutions provider to major infrastructure, industrial-plant maintenance, and construction projects best defines this business.[125]

» *Harsco Rail* was a global leader in railroad-track maintenance equipment, services, and solutions. This business was a mix of products, services, and parts. It provided leading technologies and solutions for the maintenance of rail infrastructure. The best way to define this business is as an important and essential partner to the world's railways.

» *Harsco Industrial* was a market leader in energy-efficient air-cooled heat exchangers, heat-transfer equipment, and industrial grating products. It is best defined as a manufacturing business that is number one in both air-cooled heat exchangers and industrial grating as well as a market leader in heat-transfer equipment.

As mentioned in chapter 8, "Distinctive Culture," but worth repeating here, reinvention for the company was nothing new. One of the most enduring strengths of the organization had been its ability to successfully reinvent itself since its founding. It was now time for another and possibly the most critical reinvention. In 2008, the company faced, in my view, four very specific challenges that needed to be addressed. The countermeasure to these challenges was outlined in what I would later call the CEO-envisioned future. This transformation strategy was underpinned by a strong balance sheet that had been built over decades and it was a vital lifeline for the company.

The CEO-Envisioned Future

In my mind, the need for the CEO-envisioned future was clear: the threats and risks on the horizon were becoming more visible, and an audacious transformative strategy was necessary. Let's examine in more detail each item that led to the development of the envisioned future.

1. **People:** The company went through a significant growth spurt from 2000 through 2007, driven mainly by acquisitions and the

global economic bubble. Whenever there is accelerated growth, it is difficult to grow the management talent of the organization unless there is an exceptional internal world-class management-development program. Even then it's difficult. It was my view that we needed to strengthen and augment our management talent, and thus we embarked on a comprehensive strategy to accomplish that. Simultaneously, we outlined a robust human capital framework, or talent-management and leadership-development strategy, for the long-term development of key seats.

2. **Globalization:** For a multitude of historical reasons, but principally due to acquisitions, the company over a long period of time had become a Europe-centric organization by the end of 2007. Well over half the company's revenues were generated in Europe. Consequently, London for many practical reasons had become the sister headquarters location, given the large European footprint. Although the company had a presence in some key emerging markets, there was no sustained effort to aggressively grow in these areas.

It was my view that this needed to change, and that growth in these markets had to be accelerated while the overall European concentration exposure was reduced. My objective was to rethink our model for expansion. I wanted a more innovative and dynamic approach to emerging markets, improving our exceptional capabilities and utilizing more joint ventures and strategic alliances. We focused our emerging-economies growth on the key markets of China, India, Latin America, and to a lesser extent, the Middle East.

3. **Innovation:** The company had abundant services and products serving key end-markets like metals, construction, rail, and energy. Just like any business, it is critical that management stays ahead of the competition to avoid commodity creep. Creeping commoditization should be anathema to all managers. It was my view that some commoditization would inevitably and naturally creep into parts of the business. The countermeasure

that I proposed for dealing with commodity creep was to urgently transform the enterprise into a knowledge-based solutions business underpinned by innovation, technology, and a culture of value selling.

As with the globalization strategy, I wanted to rethink our model for innovation. I envisioned utilizing an open network for innovation that included joint ventures and strategic alliances as well as other effective mechanisms. We were historically the global leader in innovation in many of our markets, and it was once again time to demonstrate our abilities and regain momentum.

4. **Optimization:** The company for many decades had successfully operated with a decentralized business model. Historically, this meant that each segment generally operated on the following structure: segment headquarters, regional headquarters, an individual country structure, and within some countries multiple branches. For countries where multiple segments operated, each had its own country/branch structure.

Operating a company built around this structure has many advantages, but the trade-off is usually higher costs. It was my belief that the decentralized model would be difficult to sustain in the future, and that it could actually be a detriment if we encountered significant headwinds (which I feared at the time based on my intuition).

These factors led to our OneHarsco initiative, the focus of which was to dramatically lower the break-even point of the company while simultaneously building new exceptional capabilities, with the objective of capturing the benefits of operating on a global scale. The OneHarsco initiative also focused on developing a unified culture.

Encountering the Perfect Economic Storm during the Ascent

Now let's get back to the perfect storm that the organization encountered early in the journey, starting in 2008. Just as most of our businesses were emerging from the US financial and economic crisis in late 2009, the infrastructure business (construction services and equipment) was starting its sharp decline due the late-cycle nature of the nonresidential construction markets. These markets usually trail the general economy by more than a year. So as other companies were slowly coming to life in 2010, Harsco was suffering even worse than in 2008–09 because the construction markets were so profoundly and negatively impacted by the crisis. Finally, in 2011, we were once again starting to gain some positive momentum and the outlook appeared somewhat promising in the early part of the year.

The storm clouds appeared to be dissipating and a ray of sunshine was on the horizon. Unfortunately, the clear weather was ephemeral. Inclement weather returned with shifting winds that brought us another severe global economic shock—the European sovereign debt crisis. It was just like 2008 but even worse because of the historical European concentration of the business. Our key end-markets suffered significant turbulence in 2011. We were again falling on the wrong side of the luck spread with a series of bad-luck events. However, the management team did some excellent work during this unprecedented period. We built a number of vital lifelines that positioned the company for the long-term.

Building Lifelines and Team Accomplishments

To provide perspective on the meaningful and measurable accomplishments and crucial lifelines that were built by the management team during the most difficult and trying period in the modern history of the company, it is important to summarize the transformational and operational accomplishments. All amounts listed below are for the period of January 1, 2008, through December 31, 2011, unless a different date is specifically stated.[126]

» *Significantly reduced costs:* The overall break-even point of the business was materially decreased by well over $230 million, and the global physical footprint of the company was substantially reduced.

» *Built exceptional capabilities*: Strategically important exceptional capabilities were built during this period, a notable investment for the future. They included a shared services competency center in India; an integrated sourcing and global supply-chain group; continuous improvement skills and know-how with Lean; and implementation of a global innovation network. In addition to these new capabilities, we notably invested in strengthening existing capabilities, including the global management team; trained key sales people on value selling; expanded research and development programs; and invested in modernizing the information-technology infrastructure. Developing new capabilities and significantly strengthening others was expensive. We cumulatively invested considerable sums to accomplish and build these lifelines.

» *Expanded emerging markets*: We invested in expanding our business in the emerging markets, with growth in revenues of approximately 50 percent in just four years—a notable achievement. At the same time, we won the largest contract in the history of the company in China with a value of approximately $500 million (2011), and we were negotiating a second contract in China for $375 million (contract was finally awarded in June 2012). We were also working hard in India for many years, and we were eventually awarded, after a long period, three separate contracts worth cumulatively approximately $500 million (announced January/February/July 2013).

» *Built rail and industrial segments*: We developed and transformed the rail and industrial segments into premier global brands; previously, they were principally US-centric businesses. Moreover, we put together a premier global minerals business that provided technology to the metals group, which also gave the company the ability to diversify its portfolio. We transformed key parts of the metals and minerals segment into an environmental-solutions company with innovative technologies.

» *Signed record number of technology agreements*: A record number of technology alliances for environmental solutions were signed in 2011. These were important lifelines for the future.

» *Successfully rebranded company*: The entire company was rebranded as Harsco across the globe.

» *Generated strong cash flow*: We averaged approximately $440 million in cash flow from operations during this period and managed to reduce debt by $172 million. In addition, we sold an assortment of miscellaneous assets for $113 million in cash. This excludes the most important asset sale, which we completed in December 2007 for over $300 million in cash when a commoditized and cyclical manufacturing business was sold. The company benefited enormously from this sale (a lifeline) because it was consummated before the economic crisis crippled the US economy.

Reflection and Perspective

Reflecting back on this period, I am reminded of the words of Henry David Thoreau: "It's not what you look at that matters, it's what you see."[127] It is interesting how some people during this period did not fully see the important foundational and transformational work that was being done and the new lifelines that were being created under severe economic constraints.

In situations like this where there are multiple global shocks and a business transformation underway, it is imperative that the CEO communicates effectively with the board of directors, the senior management team, and shareholders. Everyone needs to be aligned and clearly understand the challenges as well as the accomplishments. Leaders should not automatically assume that all parties equally understand what is truly going on. It is the CEO's responsibility to communicate often and clearly with all groups, in the same way a communication and public-relations plan is invoked during a major crisis. This is discussed in more detail in chapter 5, "Learning Entity," and is a lesson learned.

One of the ancients, Publilius Syrus, is quoted as saying, "Anyone can hold the helm when the sea is calm."[128] It is easy sailing when the economy is booming and everything is going wonderfully because you have the most important lifeline of all: a strong and healthy business environment. In this type of environment, one usually has pricing leverage and growing revenues. However, in a deep global recession, that most important lifeline is usually not there. Only the companies that are visionary and build their own multiple lifelines during good times, in anticipation of economic chaos, will normally outperform the less prepared. Without these self-created prodigious lifelines, companies that are not fully prepared for the worst-case scenario will likely suffer some pain during a severe economic disturbance.

It is important to note three rules that I believe are essential in preparing an organization for any eventuality. First, the number of self-created lifelines needs to be prodigious. (A comprehensive list of lifelines is provided in chapters 1 and 11.) Second, building and creating these lifelines must be done over a long horizon—usually several decades—and it must be embedded in the culture of the company. Third, envisioning a worst-case scenario and developing a simulation model requires a considerable team effort. The team should include senior management, economists, and outside consultants. The board also has be involved in the process.

Personal Perspective

From a professional viewpoint, this was the most difficult and personally challenging period of my career and for the company as well. We had to simultaneously deal with an unprecedented number of severe headwinds. During our ascent to the summit, the company was dramatically and adversely impacted by two extreme global economic shocks that caused considerable turbulence. Although the luck spread was materially negative, we did not deviate significantly from the CEO-envisioned future that we embarked on in 2008 when we commenced our long journey. Using the central metaphor of this book, we knew where we were in our climb and we knew how far the summit was, but we also knew that the ascent was going to be much more difficult and take longer due to the severe inclement weather.

Irrespective of all the headwinds, as a leader it is important to maintain calm and composure. This can be manifested in a variety of ways. It is also important to know that as the leader you are accountable and responsible, no matter the circumstances. The CEO is ultimately the one person who has to accept and embrace this responsibility. He cannot point to others, he cannot make excuses, and he certainly cannot ignore the situation.

Knowing and accepting responsibility is only part of the equation. The other part, which is just as critical, is how you conduct yourself with people both inside and outside the organization during the crisis. I will, of course, let others be the judge of how I conducted myself under the strain of the severe global economic shocks, but I will share my philosophy on the matter with you now.

We must all accept the cards we are dealt in life, good and bad. What is important is that we maintain a positive perspective by taking proactive actions and believing in our own abilities and character. We must also have an unwavering positive attitude and passion for the company and for all employees. As a leader or CEO, you are ultimately accountable and responsible for the results of the company and the related stock price. No matter what the consequences are, your conduct must be magnanimous, and it must be manifested with the highest integrity.

There are numerous lessons from this experience that will assist in your preparation to climb the summit that are discussed in more detail in chapter 5, "Learning Entity." In a powerful metaphor from the book *Extreme Alpinism: Climbing Light, Fast, and High*, authors Mark F. Twight and James Martin capture well the essence of the message I'm conveying:

> It makes sense to emulate the great, but don't look at their accomplishments. Instead, learn from their preparation. Focus on the mental over the physical. At some point on a climb that stretches the limits the only strength that matters is the mind.[129]

APPENDIX 2

The Power of Luck—My Journey

Be grateful for luck. Pay the thunder no mind—
listen to the birds. And don't hate nobody.
—Eubie Blake[130]

Let's examine the power of luck and how it can come in multiple forms by reviewing my personal story. Throughout this journey, many life-threatening incidents are highlighted during my youth that I survived virtually unscathed. Had even one of these unfortunate events turned out differently, my career would have most likely taken a different path. In addition to avoiding potentially fatal events, luck brought me to a better place to live—the United States.

A Whole Lot of Luck: The Early Years

In the southern Italian province of Calabria, there is a small town called Mammola that is located about twenty minutes from the Ionian Sea, facing toward Greece. This is where I was born, in a dirt basement with no doctor to oversee the delivery. It was a warm and sunny day in the summer of 1952. I was to be child number seven for my mother, Maria

Antonia. My birth, however, was anything but routine. My mother was very ill, and everyone assisting her was gravely concerned that both mother and child would not survive and make it through the delivery. Such a tragedy is unthinkable on its own, but my mother had already endured the losses of my sisters Nunzia and Rita. One died as an infant and the other at the precious age of two. So the prospect of losing another child was more than my mother could endure.

Luck, as it would be many times throughout my early life, was there for us. After a lot of praying and to everyone's relief, both my mother and I made it through the complicated and anguished birth unscathed. There was a tremendous outpouring of thanks to God by everyone assisting my mother, which led to my name of Salvatore. In Italian, Salvatore means *our savior.* Undaunted by the experience, my mother subsequently gave birth twice more, to a girl and a boy, for a total of nine children.

My memories of childhood in Mammola are mixed. On the positive side, I received tremendous love and care from my entire family but particularly from my grandmother, Maria Rosa. Also, the region was endowed with an abundance of sunshine, great beaches, and wonderful food. On the negative side, I have two particularly bad memories of Mammola that have stayed with me to this day. They occurred when I was four and five years old, before we moved to Northern Italy. Again, luck was there for me.

First, I overcame a potentially life-threatening illness when I was infected by an intestinal parasite. I inadvertently swallowed contaminated water, which caused this parasite to thrive in my body. We had no hospital and no doctor in our town, and my mother frantically searched the region for medical assistance. Lucky for me, my mother was able to find a doctor, and he was able to help me. Finding a doctor in southern Italy back then was no easy feat and was a miracle on its own. I know that my mother had to use what little money she had to get me well. I swore to myself at that point that someday I would earn enough money to not only repay her, but to give her anything she desired. I believe that I ultimately fulfilled that promise.

The second incident that I miraculously survived was a traumatic blow to the head. This happened when a child heaved a fairly large and sharp rock in my direction that I did not see. Luckily for me, the stone caught the back of my head and missed the critical areas that would have certainly killed me. I remember my head exploding with blood and pain. I fell down, stunned by the blow. Many of my neighbors and my grandmother quickly came to my assistance, and they managed to stop the bleeding. They eventually got me home. Of course, there was no doctor, so my grandmother and mother tended to my wound. Other than a scar, I made a fast and complete recovery.

In 1957, my parents decided to migrate for better economic opportunities to northern Italy, to the quaint and captivating town of Rapallo on the Ligurian Sea. Southern Italy, or *il Mezzogiorno*, was very poor and underdeveloped, with minimal job opportunities. My father had a particularly difficult time finding work in southern Italy. He often traveled in order to seek employment. Some of his travels took him to France, Canada, and ultimately to the United States. I have almost no recollection of him as a child. Northern Italy has historically been the opposite of the Mezzogiorno region in many respects. The north is economically more prosperous, driven mainly by numerous family-owned businesses and stronger tourism.

The northern Italian province of Liguria was completely different from Calabria in the south, but it seemed to be a good change for everyone in the family. We were lucky to land in a place where there were some job opportunities. Rapallo was perfectly situated on the Italian Riviera, near world-renowned Portofino and the charming and romantic town of Santa Margherita. My first year in Rapallo was memorable, but for the wrong reasons. Luck was again there for me, protecting me from the consequences of enraging my beloved mother.

With seven people to feed on a very limited budget, my mother was a master of making the most of every lira (Italian currency that was superseded by the euro) that she spent. Dinner was often determined by what she could grow in our garden and what she could acquire cheaply in the open market. We were in a period where it seemed like we were eating minestrone soup almost every night. Although today minestrone is one of my favorite meals, back when I was a kid, a soup made mostly of fresh vegetables was not too appetizing.

One day, I decided I'd had enough of the minestrone, so I sabotaged the soup by dropping candy into the pot while it was cooking. When my mother served the soup for dinner, I was the first to complain that it tasted bad, and I demanded spaghetti instead. My mother took one look at me, and I guess I must have panicked, because she saw through me. She became so enraged with me that I scrambled quickly for the door. Unfortunately, as I tried to escape the house, I tripped and went flying down the stairs. As I got up, I performed a quick scan and noted only a few cuts and bruises, so I ran as fast as I could. I did not come home that day. Somehow I was able to escape serious injury. One scar that I still carry reminds me of just how lucky I was.

The Luck Continues: A New Beginning

In the summer of 1961, my mother, two younger siblings, and I departed from the port of Genova, Italy, for the United States. My father and the older siblings emigrated to the States a year earlier. Before deciding to live permanently in America, my father visited France and Canada. He also seriously considered Argentina. Good luck was once again on my side, because my father chose the greatest country in the world: the United States. I can't imagine what my life would have been had we moved to Argentina or even France. His choice was fortuitous for me, and I am most grateful to my parents.

The ship that we traveled across the Atlantic in was very crowded, and it took eight days to make the journey. We were all clustered in a small cabin but were fortunate to survive the very tight quarters without anyone falling ill. The most memorable moment was at five in the morning when we were all awakened to go on the deck of the ship as we entered New York harbor. Seeing the majestic Statue of Liberty for the first time from a ship as a nine-year-old immigrant has left an indelible mark on me. I was completely mesmerized as we slowly made our way past her inspiring beauty. I was lucky to have such an indispensable experience at such a young age. That experience has been a driving force of my career.

After arriving in New York City, we made our way to Harrisburg, Pennsylvania, our new home. My father chose Harrisburg because his brother owned and operated a restaurant and bar in the city, and it was a perfect place for a new beginning. We arrived in America literally with nothing but the clothes on our backs. We were the typical European immigrants: poor but proud, with a strong family and work ethic.

Since we arrived in the United States in late summer, school was right around the corner. My mother had to literally drag me to elementary school because I had no interest in attending. The principal put me in a class with a number of kids from my new neighborhood, including my new best friend, which helped immensely with my orientation to American schools. The first couple of months were difficult, but I learned the English language quickly and by Christmas I was already fluent and well-acclimated. I was fortunate to learn English at a young age, because it was an important first step on my long journey to the summit.

After I graduated from high school, I worked in order to help my family financially and to save for a car. At that time, I believed college was not possible for me, so I gave it little thought. A year after I graduated, I was lucky to have the opportunity to spend the summer in Italy with relatives, including my grandmother. This was my first trip back to Italy since we left the country. The most important thing about that summer was that it opened my eyes to the need to go to college and earn a degree. I was amazed by how knowledgeable my relatives were about world events. I was fortunate to have a few cousins who were highly intelligent, and I spent the entire summer in great dialogue with them. This was a period of considerable personal enlightenment and growth.

Luck was once again on my side, because that summer in Italy totally transformed me in all respects. Someone was clearly looking out for me; I was put on the right path. I came back to the United States more mature, more knowledgeable, and more European than when I left Italy at the age of nine. I knew all along that my destiny was in business, and I finally took the most important step at the end of the summer of 1972 to realizing my dream: I enrolled in college.

I was also fortunate to spend a second summer in Italy while I was attending college. That summer of 1976, I needed luck to rescue me one more time. I was at the beach with my brother and my cousin. The water was deceptively shallow for several feet, and then suddenly, the water depth increased from three feet to thirty feet. I knew this because of my fear of water, but that day I did not pay particular attention to where I was walking. When I took a step too far, I suddenly noticed that I could no longer touch bottom. This is a feeling you do not want to experience, particularly if you are terrified of water.

Of course I panicked as I was going down. Luckily, my brother and cousin, who were both terrific swimmers, saw what was going on and came after me. They pulled me up and tried to calm me, but in my panic I pulled them both down with me as they struggled to control the situation. Meanwhile, another young man saw what was happening, and he too came to the rescue. It took all three of them to get me back to shore. Since that day, I have not stepped in water deeper than a couple of feet.

I am grateful for the positive luck events in my early life that put me on the right path. Without positive luck spread and a multitude of indispensable experiences at such a young age, I would have never had the opportunity to be in the position to climb my professional summit.

NOTES

1. "John Quincy Adams," BrainyQuote, http://www.brainyquote.com/quotes/quotes/j/johnquincy386752.html.

2. "Vincent Van Gogh," BrainyQuote, http://www.brainyquote.com/quotes/quotes/v/vincentvan120866.html.

3. George Oldfield, Michael Cragg, and Jehan deFonseka, "Understanding the Credit Crisis Part 2: Getting Down the Mountain," *Finance 2,* The Brattle Group, 2009.

4. Anatoli Boukreev and G. Weston DeWalt, *The Climb: Tragic Ambitions on Everest* (New York: St. Martin's Griffin, 1997), xv.

5. Ronald C. Eng, ed., *Mountaineering: The Freedom of the Hills,* 8th Edition (Seattle: The Mountaineers Books, 2010), 17.

6. "Albert Einstein," BrainyQuote, http://www.brainyquote.com/quotes/quotes/a/alberteins100659.htm.

7. Eng, *Mountaineering,* 474–77.

8. "Agatha Christie Quotes," GoodReads, http://www.goodreads.com/quotes/159789.htm.

9. "John Sununu," BrainyQuote, http://www.brainyquote.com/quotes/quotes/j/johnsununu451255.html.

10. Gary Wolf, "Steve Jobs: The Next Insanely Great Thing," *Wired,* http://www.wired.com/wired/archive/4.02/jobs_pr.html.

11. "Clara Barton," BrainyQuote, http://www.brainyquote.com/quotes/quotes/c/clarabarto276766.html.

12. "Herbert Hoover," BrainyQuote, http://www.brainyquote.com/quotes/quotes/h/herberthoo386232.html.

13. John Kador, *Effective Apology: Mending Fences, Building Bridges, and Restoring Trust* (San Francisco: Barrett-Koehler, 2009), 5, 6, 11.

14. "Mark Twain," BrainyQuote, http://www.brainyquote.com/quotes/quotes/m/marktwain169487.html.

15. Mark Houston and Kathy Cosley, *Alpine Climbing: Techniques to Take You Higher* (Seattle: The Mountaineers Books, 2004), 22.

16. "Inspirational Quotes," Belief.Net, http://www.beliefnet.com/Quotes/Inspiration/R/Ronald-Reagan/Every-New-Day-Begins-With-Possibilities-Its-Up-T.aspx.

17. "C. S. Lewis," BrainyQuote, http://www.brainyquote.com/quotes/quotes/c/cslewis395865.html.

18. Fred Thompson, "What Made Ronald Reagan the Great Communicator: Former US Senator Fred Thompson Reflects," *Daily News,* February 6, 2011, http://www.nydailynews.com/opinion/made-ronald-reagan-great-communicator-u-s-senator-fred-thompson-reflects-article-1.133489.

19. Houston and Cosley, *Alpine Climbing,* 15.

20. "Mark Twain," BrainyQuote, http://www.brainyquote.com/quotes/quotes/m/marktwain118739.html.

21. Geoff Colvin, "The Economy Is Scary, But Smart Companies Can Still Dominate," *Fortune,* September 24, 2012, 77.

22. Anupreeta Das, "Buffett's Crisis-Lending Haul Reaches $10 Billion," *Wall Street Journal,* October 7, 2013, A1–A2.

23. Mark F. Twight and James Martin, *Extreme Alpinism: Climbing Light, Fast, and High* (Seattle: The Mountaineers Books, 1999), 20.

24. "Melody Beattie," BrainyQuote, http://www.brainyquote.com/quotes/quotes/m/melodybeat134462.html.

25. "Thomas Edison," BrainyQuote, http://www.brainyquote.com/quotes/quotes/t/thomasaed149049.html.

26. "Jack Welch," BrainyQuote, http://www.brainyquote.com/quotes/quotes/j/jackwelch173305.html.

27. Houston and Cosley, *Alpine Climbing*, 17.

28. "Lao Tzu," BrainyQuote, http://www.brainyquote.com/quotes/quotes/l/laotzu137141.html.

29. Houston and Cosley, *Alpine Climbing*, 30–31.

30. "Albert Einstein," BrainyQuote, http://www.brainyquote.com/quotes/quotes/a/alberteins148778.html.

31. "Julius Caesar," BrainyQuote, http://www.brainyquote.com/quotes/quotes/j/juliuscaes398606.html.

32. Louis V. Gerstner Jr., *Who Says Elephants Can't Dance?* (New York: HarperCollins, 2002), cover jacket.

33. Ibid., 2–5.

34. Ibid., 3.

35. Ibid., 5.

36. Salvatore Fazzolari, "How Harsco Integrates Financial and Operational Auditing," *Management Accounting*, January 1988, 28–31.

37. "Thomas Jefferson," BrainyQuote, http://www.brainyquote.com/quotes/quotes/t/thomasjeff120901.html.

38. James M. Citrin, "So … Do You Still Want to Be a CEO," *The Conference Board Review*, May/June 2009, 41–44.

39. Martin Lipton, Steven A. Rosenblum, Karessa L. Cain, and Kendal Y. Fox, "Some Thoughts for Board of Directors in 2013," December 1, 2012, http://www.wlrk.com/docs/SomeThoughtsforBoardsofDirectorsin2013.pdf.

40. Nicolas Rapp, "Tenure at the Top," *Fortune*, October 29, 2012, 28.

41. Ken Favaro, Per-Ola Karlsson, Jon Katzenbach, and Gary Neilson, "Lessons from the Trenches for New CEOs: Separating Myths from Game Changers," Booz & Company, 2010.

42. "Ronald Reagan," BrainyQuote, http://www.brainyquote.com/quotes/quotes/r/ronaldreag147717.html.

43. Michael E. Porter, Jay W. Lorsch, and Nitin Nohria, "Seven Surprises for New CEOs," *Harvard Business Review*, October 2004.

44. "Watch Your Thoughts, They Become Words; Watch Your Words, They Become Actions," *Quote Investigator,* http://quoteinvestigator. com/2013/01/10/watch-your-thoughts/.

45. Nassim Nicholas Taleb, *The Black Swan: The Impact of the Highly Improbable* (New York: Random House, 2007), 161–62.

46. Twight and Martin, *Extreme Alpinism,* 138.

47. Walter Isaacson, *Steve Jobs* (New York: Simon & Schuster, 2011), 334.

48. Jim Collins and Morton Hansen, *Great by Choice* (New York: HarperCollins, 2011), 147.

49. Michael Porter, "What Is Strategy?" *Harvard Business Review,* 1996.

50. Houston and Cosley, *Alpine Climbing,* 71–80.

51. Roper Industries, Inc., 2010 Annual Report, February 25, 2011, 6, downloaded from http://phx.corporate-ir.net/phoenix. zhtml?c=99690&p=irol-reportsannual.

52. Isaacson, *Steve Jobs,* 408.

53. "George Bernard Shaw," BrainyQuote, http://www.brainyquote.com/ quotes/quotes/g/georgebern121841.html.

54. Houston and Cosley, *Alpine Climbing,* 25.

55. "John F. Kennedy," BrainyQuote, http://www.brainyquote.com/quotes/ quotes/j/johnfkenn130752.html.

56. Twight and Martin, *Extreme Alpinism,* 25.

57. "Minna Antrim," BrainyQuote, http://www.brainyquote.com/quotes/ quotes/m/minnaantri109746.html.

58. "Winston Churchill," BrainyQuote, http://www.brainyquote.com/quotes/ quotes/w/winstonchu135270.html.

59. Rich Cohen, "Five Lessons from the Banana Man," *Wall Street Journal,* June 1, 2012, http://online.wsj.com/news/articles/SB10001424052702303640 104577436372487764502.

60. Ian Bremmer, *Every Nation for Itself* (New York: Penquin Group, 2012), 126.

61. Jeffrey J. Selingo, *College (Un)bound* (New York: Houghton Mifflin Harcourt Publishing Company, 2013), 67.

62. Twight and Martin, *Extreme Alpinism,* 22.

63. Richard A. D'Aveni, *Beating the Commodity Trap* (Boston: Harvard Business Press, 2010), 41.

64. Bob Tita, "Crane Industry Waits for Recovery," *Wall Street Journal,* July 26, 2013, B6.

65. Brian O'Keefe, "Lessons from Coach Saban," *Fortune,* September 24, 2012, 158.

66. "Aristotle," BrainyQuote, http://www.brainyquote.com/quotes/quotes/a/aristotle145967.html.

67. Adam Lashinsky, *Inside Apple* (New York: Business Plus, Hachette Book Group, 2012), 58.

68. Isaacson, *Steve Jobs,* 370.

69. Tony Chapelle, "A Sneak Preview of the Agenda Digital 50 Guide," *Agenda,* November 4, 2013, 12–13.

70. Jim Collins, *Good to Great* (New York: HarperCollins, 2001), 54.

71. Collins, *Great by Choice,* 65.

72. Jack Welch, with John A. Byrne, *Jack: Straight from the Gut* (New York: Business Plus, 2001), 158.

73. Stephen Ambrose, *Undaunted Courage* (New York: Simon & Schuster, 1996), cover jacket.

74. Twight and Martin, *Extreme Alpinism,* 40–42.

75. Jim Collins, *Where Are You on Your Journey from Good to Great?: Good to Great Diagnostic Tool,* Release Version 1.0 (Boulder, CO: The Good to Great Project LLC, 2006), http://www.jimcollins.com/tools/diagnostic-tool.pdf, 4.

76. Welch and Byrne, *Straight from the Gut,* 158–60.

77. Shira Ovide and Rachel Feinzeig, "Microsoft Abandons 'Stack Ranking' of Employees," *Wall Street Journal,* November 12, 2013, http://online.wsj.com/news/articles/SB10001424052702303460004579193951987616572.

78. Rachel Emma Silverman and Lauren Weber, "An Inside Job: More Firms Opt to Recruit from Within," *Wall Street Journal,* May 30, 2012, http://online.wsj.com/article/SB10001424052702303395604577434563715828218.

79. Vickie Elmer, "Avoid Hiring the Unexpected," *Fortune,* September 24, 2012, 45.

80. Patricia Sellers, "Marissa Mayer: Ready to Rumble at Yahoo," *Fortune,* October 29, 2013, 120.

81. Eng, *Mountaineering,* 16.

82. Gerstner, *Who Says Elephants Can't Dance?,* 182.

83. Fred Hassan, *Reinvent: A Leader's Playbook for Serial Success* (Hoboken, NJ: Jossey-Bass, 2013), 3.

84. Collins, *Where Are You on Your Journey from Good to Great?,* 4.

85. "William E. Simon Quotes," SearchQuotes, http://www.searchquotes.com/quotes/author/William_E_Simon/.

86. "Abraham Lincoln Quotes," GoodReads, http://www.goodreads.com/quotes/340549-commitment-is-what-transforms-a-promise-into-reality.

87. Favaro, Karlsson, Katzenbach, and Neilson. "Lessons from the Trenches for New CEOs." 2010, Booz & Company Inc., page 8.

88. RPM International Inc., 2012 Annual Report.

89. Roper Industries, Inc., 2012 Annual Report.

90. Jim Collins and Jerry I. Porras, *Built to Last* (New York: HarperCollins, 2004), 67.

91. Jim Collins and Jerry I. Porras, "Building Your Company's Vision," *Harvard Business Review,* 1996.

92. Ibid.

93. "Our Values," IBM, http://www-03.ibm.com/employment/our_values.html.

94. Ibid.

95. Ibid.

96. "Leading Through Connections: Insights from the Global Chief Executive Officer Study," IBM Corporation, 2012, 24.

97. Collins and Porras, "Building Your Company's Vision." *Harvard Business Review,* 1996.

98. "Company," Google, http://www.google.com/about/company/.

99. Barbara Farfan, "eBay Corporate Mission Statement—Global, Social, Entrepreneurial, and Virtual," About.com Retail Industry, http://retailindustry.about.com/od/retailbestpractices/ig/Company-Mission-Statements/eBay-Corporate-Mission-Statement.htm.

100. "About Southwest," Southwest Airlines, http://www.southwest.com/html/about-southwest/index.html.

101. "Company Overview," Union Pacific, http://www.up.com/aboutup/corporate_info/uprrover/index.htm.

102. "Our Company," The Coca-Cola Company, http://www.coca-colacompany.com/our-company/mission-vision-values.

103. "About," Facebook, https://www.facebook.com/facebook/info.

104. "Hearst History," Hearst Corporation, http://www.hearst.com/about-hearst/history.php.

105. "What Is Singularity University?," Singularity University, http://singularityu.org/.

106. "Core Values," Danaher, http://www.danaher.com/core-values.

107. "Napoleon Bonaparte," BrainyQuote, http://www.brainyquote.com/quotes/quotes/n/napoleonbo163758.html.

108. Twight and James, *Extreme Alpinism*, 21.

109. "Peter Drucker," BrainyQuote, http://www.brainyquote.com/quotes/quotes/p/peterdruck131600.html.

110. "Shirley Temple Black," BrainyQuote, http://www.brainyquote.com/quotes/quotes/s/shirleytem380631.html.

111. Taleb, *The Black Swan*, 105–6.

112. Henry Mintzberg, "No More Executive Bonuses!" *Wall Street Journal*, November 30, 2009.

113. Dr. Richard Wiseman, *The Luck Spread* (London: Century, 2002), 11–12.

114. Collins, *Great by Choice*, 178.

115. Jim Collins, *How the Mighty Fall* (New York: HarperCollins, 2009), 44.

116. Harding Loevner, Annual Commentary, October 31, 2012, http://www.hardingloevnerfunds.com/fileadmin/pdf/HLF/Annual-Report-2012.pdf.

117. Ryan Bradley, "Working Glass," *Fortune,* May 20, 2013.

118. A. G. Lafley and Roger L. Martin, *Playing to Win: How Strategy Really Works* (Boston: Harvard Business Review Press, 2013), 71.

119. Anatoli Boukreev and G. Weston DeWalt, *The Climb: Tragic Ambitions on Everest* (New York: St. Martin's Griffin, 1999), 255–58.

120. Dr. Richard Wiseman, *The Luck Factor* (London: Century, 2002), 168–69.

121. "Thomas Jefferson Encyclopedia," Thomas Jefferson's Monticello, http://www.monticello.org/site/research-and-collections/i-am-great-believer-luckquotation.

122. "Theodore Roosevelt," BrainyQuote, http://www.brainyquote.com/quotes/quotes/t/theodorero120908.html.

123. "Albert Einstein," BrainyQuote, http://www.brainyquote.com/quotes/quotes/a/alberteins118979.html.

124. Eng, *Mountaineering,* 8.

125. On September 17, 2013, Harsco announced in a press release that it was selling the infrastructure business into a joint venture with the private equity firm Clayton, Dubilier & Rice. The completion of this transaction was announced in a press release dated November 26, 2013.

126. All information is from public documents, including annual reports, form 10-K, company press releases, and investor presentations.

127. "Henry David Thoreau," BrainyQuote, http://www.brainyquote.com/quotes/quotes/h/henrydavid106041.html.

128. "Publilius Syrus," BrainyQuote, http://www.brainyquote.com/quotes/quotes/p/publiliuss136056.html.

129. Twight and Martin, *Extreme Alpinism,* 20.

130. "Eubie Blake," BrainyQuote, http://www.brainyquote.com/quotes/quotes/e/eubieblake131386.html.

ABOUT THE AUTHOR

Salvatore D. Fazzolari is the president and chief executive officer of Salvatore Fazzolari Advisors LLC. He is the former chairman, president, and CEO of Harsco Corporation. Currently he is a board member of RPM International Inc., a world leader in specialty coatings, sealants, building products, and related services serving both industrial and consumer markets; Gannett Fleming Affiliates Inc., a global engineering company; and Bollman Hat Company, a world leading designer, manufacturer, and distributor of men's, women's, and children's headwear and accessories. He is also a trustee of Susquehanna University, a private liberal-arts university located in Pennsylvania.

He has published an article in *Management Accounting* magazine (1988) and had a short essay published in Dr. Richard A. D'Aveni's book *Strategic Capitalism: The New Economic Strategy for Winning the Capitalist Cold War* (2012). Salvatore is currently working on a second book, on Italian cuisine and culture. He is also acknowledged by Jim Collins in two books: *Great by Choice* and *How the Mighty Fall.*

He has extensive public speaking experience at universities, investor conferences, companies, and national conferences.

INDEX

A

acclimation, importance of, 63, 64

accountability

    executive accountability, 95

as fully and squarely on CEO's shoulders, 52

as key core value, 165, 197

as personal characteristic of right people, 136, 192

as precocious characteristic, 5, 18, 182

acquisitions

    importance of integrating immediately, 100, 189

    targeting strategic ones, 111, 125–126, 191

actions, employment of to deal with CEO surprises (proactive action), 54–55

Adams, John Quincy, ix

Agenda (Financial Times), 122

Alpine Climbing: Techniques to Take You Higher (Houston and Cosley), 9, 20, 24, 67, 77

Alsever, Jennifer, 122

Ambrose, Stephen, 131

American Express, 28, 29

AMP (now TE Connectivity), 33

antidotes, employment of to deal with CEO surprises (proactive action), 54–55

Antrim, Minna, 80

A-players/A-team, xvii, 18, 83, 84, 85, 116, 132, 133, 140, 163, 184, 188, 192, 197, 198

apologize, willingness to (precocious characteristic), 4, 8–9

Apple, 6, 7, 70, 72, 114, 119, 132, 174
appropriate training, for new CEOs, 27
Aristotle, 109
assessments
 of lifelines, 42
 of people characteristics, 85–86, 139
 of risk, 200
 of skills and knowledge, 20–21
author's career lifelines, 29–32
author's journey
 from the beginning, 30–31
 connections to China, 35, 125
 connections to leading business experts, 36
 first senior-management exposure, 32–34
 key indispensable experiences, 35–37
 living the American dream, 31
 new summits to climb after Harsco, 36–37
 personal lifelines developed through proactive actions, 43–45
"Avoid Hiring the Unexpected," 142

B

backlog
 development of (proactive action), 56–57
 monitoring of, 121
balance sheets, rebuilding of, 95–96
Barton, Clara, 7
Bartz, Carol, 145
Beating the Commodity Trap (D'Aveni), 47, 98
Beattie, Melody, 17
Black, Shirley Temple, 172
The Black Swan (Taleb), 57, 172
Blake, Eubie, 221
board membership, as personal lifeline, 58
board of directors support, for new CEOs, 27
board-related matters, lessons learned, 103–106
boards
 connections of CEO to that need to be managed, 51–53
 importance of CEOs joining other boards, 27, 42, 43, 58, 106–107
 key responsibilities of, 201–202

understanding role of (proactive action), 50–53

Bonaparte, Napoleon, 169

Booz & Company, 49, 148

Boukreev, Anatoli, xix, 176

B-player, 132

brand development, focus on, 119

Bremmer, Ian, 47, 91

Buffett, Warren, 14–15, 24

"Building Your Company's Vision," 158

Built to Last (Collins and Porras), 46, 158

business enterprises, reaching highest summit in, 62–64

business leaders, new breed of, 4–20

business model

    centralized (fully integrated), 69, 70–71, 75, 186

    characteristics of successful ones, 72–73

    decentralized, 69, 75, 186

    effective business framework, 74–75

    hybrid (matrix), 69, 70, 75, 186

    as one of six practices of healthy enterprise, 61, 65–76

    organizational structure component, 66, 69–71

    recipe component, 66–68

    results of effective/innovative one, 71–72

    summary of, 186–187

    variable cost model, 117–118

    business portfolio, importance of evaluating early in tenure, 94

Byrne, John, 15

C

capital efficiency, improvement of, 112–113

career-building experiences, 24–25

case studies, of indispensable experiences, 28–29

cash-conversion cycle, enhancement of, 112

centralized (fully integrated) business model, 69, 70–71, 75, 186

CEO relationship, establishment of (proactive action), 50–53

CEO surprises, 54–55

CEOs

    actions newly appointed CEOs need to take, 45–47

    don't assume everyone will be like you, 81

    job is not to make friends, 81

leadership tenure as ephemeral, 40–41

providing essential leadership lifelines to new CEOs, 26–27

role of as combined or separate from chairman, 105–106

ten critical proactive actions for newly appointed CEOs, 48–58

ten rules to live by, 203

chairman, role of as combined or separate from CEO, 105–106

change

importance of thinking differently and adapting to, 91–92

manage change well, 87–88

pursuit of with patience, wisdom, and high level of skepticism (proactive action), 53

Chapelle, Tony, 122

chief human-resources officer (CHRO), 46, 83

China, author's connections to, 35, 125

Christie, Agatha, 6

Churchill, Winston, 81

Clark, William, 132

Climb the Summit: Harsco's Ascent from Good to Great, 152

Climbing Code (in mountaineering), xix–xx

The Climb: Tragic Ambitions on Everest (Boukreev and DeWalt), xix, 176

coaching ability (precocious characteristic), 5, 19–20

Coca-Cola

building brand through downturn, 13

mission statement as exemplary, 164, 196

"Coffee with the Chairman," 55

Cohen, Rich, 91

College (Un)bound (Selingo), 97

Collins, Jim, 36, 45, 46, 55, 66, 67, 127, 133, 146, 151, 157, 158, 160, 173, 176

Colvin, Geoff, 13

communication plans, create effective ones, 88

communication skills (precocious characteristic), 5, 11

competition, importance of not focusing primarily on, 100–101

Conference Board Review, 40

Connect and Develop model (Procter & Gamble), 120

consistency, as personal characteristic of right people, 136

continuous self-improvement (precocious characteristic), 5, 16

core ideology, 158–159

core philosophy

as one of six practices of healthy enterprise, 61, 157–166

summary of, 195

core values
core philosophy as built around mission statement and core values, 157, 195
    Economic Value Added (EVA), 56
    examples of, 196–197
    good fit with, as personal characteristic of right people, 134, 135–136, 192
    of Harsco, 135, 152, 162–163, 197
    IBM's codification of, 159–160, 165, 196
    Lean or Six-Sigma as recommended core value, 114
    menu of possible ones, 164–165, 196–197
    as never changing, 159
    as part of winning culture, 86
    safety, 55, 185
    of Salvatore Fazzolari Advisors LLC, 161
    value creation, 127
Corning, example of positive luck spread, 174
Cosley, Kathy, 9, 11, 20, 24, 67, 77
cost mind-set (precocious characteristic), 5, 13
Costa Rica, as ideal place for global shared services, 114
courage (precocious characteristic), 5, 12–13
C-players, 141
Cragg, Michael, xix
culture
CEO perspective on, 146
create a winning culture, 86
    key elements of distinctive culture, 148–149
culture of discipline, 146–147
customer, focus on (proactive action), 48–49

D

Danaher, core values of, 164–165, 196
Das, Anupreeta, 14
D'Aveni, Richard A., 36, 47, 98
Deadly Summit, xix
death, threat of in business, 64
Death Zone, xix
decentralized business model, 69, 75, 186
deFoneska, Jehan, xix
determine where true economic value is created (proactive action), 55–56
DeWalt, G. Weston, xix, 176

discipline
    culture of, 146–147
    as precocious characteristic, 4, 7
disciplined growth, maintenance of, 127–128
distinctive culture
    examples of, 153
    key elements of, 148–149
    as one of six practices of healthy enterprise, 61, 145–155
    summary of, 194
Drucker, Peter, 171

E

Eastern civilization, author's study of, 44
eBay, mission statement as exemplary, 163, 195
economic turbulence, dealing decisively with, 97–99
Economic Value Added (EVA), 55, 101–103, 112–113, 127–128
Edison, Thomas, 19
Effective Apology: Mending Fences, Building Bridges, and Restoring Trust
    (Kador), 8
Einstein, Albert, 3, 25, 209
enduring enterprise
    ability to build (precocious characteristic), 5, 13–14
    investment in building of, 14
Eng, Ronald C., xix–xx, 3
enterprise excellence, how nine lifelines fit together to promote, xviii
enterprise-resource planning (ERP) system, 70, 122
environmental scan, importance of real-time scan, 121–122
envisioned future, development of (proactive action), 49–50
equanimity (precocious characteristic), 5, 17
ethics, as personal characteristic of right people, 134–135
Every Nation for Itself (Bremmer), 47, 91
exceptional capabilities
    list of, 110–111
    as one of six practices of healthy enterprise, 61, 109–129
    summary of, 190–191
exceptional leaders, list of descriptors, 21
execution
    and focus, lessons learned, 100–103
    good execution (precocious characteristic), 5, 10–11

executive retreat, as mechanism of learning entity, 79
executive team support, for new CEOs, 27
extensive training, as indispensable experiences, 26
Extreme Alpinism: Climbing Light, Fast, and High (Twight and Martin), 16, 63, 78, 97, 132, 170, 219

F

Facebook, mission statement as exemplary, 164, 196
Financial Times, 122
first aid, importance of, 64
FMC Corporation, 124–125
focus on customer (proactive action), 48–49
follow-through, as personal characteristic of right people, 136
forecasting
    development of system for (proactive action), 56–57
    monitoring of, 121
Fortune 500 companies, 64
Fortune magazine, 13, 40, 41, 122, 142, 174
foundation, strong, building of, 132–133
free-cash-flow calculations, 73–74
frontier markets, identification of, 128
fully integrated (centralized) business model, 69, 70–71, 75, 186

G

General Electric (GE)
    talent-management system, 120, 140–141
    transformation of, 15
    generative thinking
    of IBM, 159–160
    as precocious characteristic, 5, 15–16
Gerstner, Louis V., Jr., 28–29, 47, 141, 146, 159
giving nature (precocious characteristic), 5, 18
global leadership team
    bringing together (proactive action), 58
    definition of, 137–138
global legal/tax structure, 118
global shared services/shared global services, 12, 70, 89, 110, 114, 190
global shocks, dealing decisively with, 97–99
global supply chain, use of integrated one, 110, 113–114, 190

globalization
>   as one of three Harsco initiatives, 87
>   as philosophical strategy, 111, 127–128, 190
good execution (precocious characteristic), 5, 10–11
Good to Great (Collins), 46, 55, 127, 146, 151, 154
Google
>   as example of company organized/structured around products, 116
>   mission statement as exemplary, 163, 195
gratefulness (precocious characteristic), 5, 17
Great by Choice (Collins), 36, 46, 66, 127, 146, 151, 173, 176
growth, disciplined, maintenance of, 127–128
growth and inner reflection, importance of allowing for, 82–83
growth capital, 73–74

H

Harding Loevner, 173
Harrisburg Steel, 31
Harsco
>   author as CEO of, 12, 19, 27, 32
>   author as CFO of, 33
>   author as president of, 34
>   author's hire at, 31
>   beginnings of, 31
>   business-model search, 70
>   core values of, 135, 152, 161–162, 197
>   culture of, 149–153
>   as EVA company, 127
>   as example of negative luck spread, 175–176
>   fiftieth anniversary celebration, 34
>   identification of personal characteristics of right people, 133
>   key-seats leadership team, 137
>   mission statement, 196
>   OneHarsco initiative, 45, 87, 89–91, 150, 152
>   three initiatives of, 87
>   transformation story, 209–219
Harsco Industrial, 93
Harsco Internal Control Framework (Fazzolari), 33
Harsco Minerals, 93
Harsco Rail, 93

Harvard Business Review, 43, 54–55, 120, 158, 160
Hassan, Fred, 47, 146
healthy enterprises, six practices of, overview, 61–64
Hearst Corporation, mission statement as exemplary, 164, 196
Hewlett Packard (HP), 6, 127
high results, delivering of, as personal characteristic of right people, 135
hiring, promote from within and limit senior-management-level outside hires, 84
Hoover, Herbert, 8
hope for the best, but plan for the worst, 99
Houston, Mark, 9, 11, 20, 24, 67, 77
How the Mighty Fall (Collins), 36, 46, 151, 173
humility (precocious characteristic), 5, 11
Huston, Larry, 120
hybrid (matrix) business model, 69, 70, 75, 186
Hyderabad, as ideal place for global shared services, 114

I

IBM
    as example of core value transformation, 159–160, 165, 196
    Louis V. Gerstner Jr. as CEO of, 141, 146
    talent-management system, 120
    transformation of, 28
IKEA, 67
India, as ideal place for global shared services, 114
indispensable experiences
    case studies of, 28–29
    as one of three practices for sustained leadership, 1, 23–37
    summary of, 183
information technology (IT)
infrastructure of, 70
    as strategic asset, 122–123
inner reflection and growth, importance of allowing for, 82–83
innovation
investment in, 119–120
    as one of three Harsco initiatives, 87
    as philosophical strategy, 111, 119–126, 190
inquisitiveness (precocious characteristic), 5, 12
instincts (precocious characteristic), 4, 6, 80

integrated supply-chain management, 70, 89, 100, 186, 198

integrity

as personal characteristic of right people, 134–135

as precocious characteristic, 4, 5–6

internal university, as mechanism of learning entity, 79

investments

in building enduring enterprises, 14

in high-capital expenditure businesses, careful consideration of, 92–93

investors, meet with (proactive action), 48–49

Isaacson, Walter, 6, 47, 66, 70

Isshin-Ryu Karate, 43–44

J

Jack: Straight from the Gut (Byrne), 15, 47, 140

Jefferson, Thomas, 39, 131, 132, 178

Jobs, Steve, 6, 7, 14, 65, 66, 119, 132, 174

joint ventures

importance of seeking out, 124–125

as mechanism of learning entity, 79–80

Julius Caesar, 25

K

Kador, John, 8

Kaizen Breakthrough Event, 115, 196

Kennedy, John F., 78

key performance metric, development of (proactive action), 49–50

key-seats leadership team, 137–138

Khan Academy, 97

L

Lafley, A. G., 47, 174

Lao Tzu, 23

Lashinsky, Adam, 114

leadership-development practice, innovation in, 140

Lean continuous-improvement discipline, 12–13, 70, 89, 91, 110, 112, 113, 114–115, 163, 186, 190, 198

learning, teaching, and coaching ability (precocious characteristic), 5, 19–20

learning committee, as mechanism of learning entity, 79

learning entity
    essential elements of, 79–80
    as one of six practices of healthy enterprise, 61, 77–108
    summary of, 188–189
legal/tax structure, global, 118
lessons learned
    about learning entities
    board-related matters, 103–106
    execution and focus, 100–103
    people excellence, 83–87
    personal characteristics, 80–83
    uncertainty and turbulence, 97–99
    about transformation and reinvention, 87–97
Lewis, C. S., 11
Lewis, Meriwether, 131–132
Lewis and Clark expedition, 131
lifelines
    for new CEOs 26–27
    inventory of, 20–21, 128–129
    self-created enterprise, 198
    value of, xviii
    what they demonstrate, xvii
Lincoln, Abraham, 17, 147
Lipton, Martin, 40
loyalty (precocious characteristic), 4, 9
luck
    four principles of, according to Richard Wiseman, 177–178
    Jim Collins on, 173
    Nassim Nicholas Taleb on, 172
    power of, author's journey, 221–226
    Richard Wiseman on, 172, 177–178
    Shirley Temple Black on, 172
    the wild card of a CEO's success, 167
    as wild card of a CEO's success, 169–179
luck factor, and nine lifelines, 177–178
luck spread, xvi–xvii, 63, 133, 169, 170–179, 181, 207
The Luck Factor (Wiseman), 172, 177

M

Magretta, Joan, 46
maintenance and growth capital, 73–74
major restructuring actions, importance of being audacious when undertaking, 94–95
Management Accounting magazine, 32
Manufacturers Alliance for Productivity and Innovation (MAPI), 44
Markkula, Mike, 119
Martin, James, 16, 63, 78, 97, 132, 170, 219
Martin, Roger L., 174
matrix (hybrid) business model, 69, 70, 75, 186
maturity, importance of, 63
McDonald's, 96
McKinsey & Company, 28, 29
mechanisms, summary of, 199
mentoring
    as indispensable experiences, 26
    for new CEOs, 26–27
metaphors, use of, ix, x, xv–xvi, xviii–xix, 23, 63, 78, 145, 170, 209, 218, 219
MetLife, use of technology by, 122
metrics, importance of not relying on single metric, 101
Microsoft, 96
mission statements, examples of, 163–164
Motorola, 33, 115
mountaineering metaphors. *See also* metaphors, use of
    getting up the mountain is optional, getting down the mountain is
        mandatory, xix
    hope for the best, but plan for the worst, xix
Mountaineering: The Freedom of the Hills (Eng), xix–xx, 3, 145, 209

N

national organizations, value of joining, 44
navigational skills (precocious characteristic), 4, 9–10
negative luck-spread examples, 175–176
negotiating skills (precocious characteristic), 5, 17
net operating profit after-tax (NOPAT), 101
niche businesses, investing and growing, 93–94

O

Oldfield, George, xix
OneHarsco initiative, 45, 87, 89–91, 150–153, 214
optimism (precocious characteristic), 4, 10
optimization
    as one of three Harsco initiatives, 87
    as philosophical strategy, 111–119, 190
organizations, national, value of joining, 44
Outlaw, Frank, 54–55
outside hires, promote from within and limit senior-management-level outside
    hires, 84–85
outside relationship with trusted confidant, for new CEOs, 27
overseas experience, as indispensable experiences, 26

P

Packard, David, 127
Packard's law, 127
Palmisano, Samuel J., 159
passion
    for company's culture, as personal characteristic of right people, 136
    as precocious characteristic, 4, 10
patience, pursuit of change with (proactive action), 53
Pennsylvania State University (Harrisburg), author's connections to, 44
pension plans, restructuring of, 96
people, treatment of, treat all people equally and with respect, 82
people characteristics, importance of establishing appropriate mechanisms to
    embed and assess, 85–86
people excellence
    lessons learned, 83–87
    as one of six practices of healthy enterprise, 61, 131–143
    summary of, 192–193
performance metric, key, development of (proactive action), 49–50
perseverance (precocious characteristic), 5, 18–19
personal characteristics
    alternative framework for assessment of, 139
    lessons learned, 80–83
    of right people, 133–138
personal excellence, how nine lifelines fit together to promote, xviii
perspective (precocious characteristic), 4, 7

philosophical strategies, exceptional capabilities as classified into, 111

Playing to Win: How Strategy Really Works (Lafley), 47, 174

Porras, Jerry, 157, 158, 160

Porter, Michael, 46–47, 66, 67

position/reputation, importance of being proactive in protecting, 81–82

positive luck spread examples, 174–175, 208

postevent debrief, as mechanism of learning entity, 79

precocious characteristics

    list of, 4–5

    as one of three practices for sustained leadership, 1, 3–21

    summary of, 182

pricing power, taking advantage of, 116–117

pride, in company's culture, as personal characteristic of right people, 136

proactive, ability to be (precocious characteristic), 5, 11

proactive actions

    importance of being proactive in protecting position/reputation, 81–82

    as one of three practices for sustained leadership, 1, 39–59

    overview and need for, 42–43

    recipe for success through, 41–42

    summary of, 184–185

    ten critical ones for newly appointed CEOs, 48–58

Procter & Gamble (P&G)

    Connect and Develop model, 120

    as example of positive luck spread, 174–175

    talent-management system, 120

product-management strategy, execution of, 115–116

Progressive Insurance, 67

project-management skills, development of, 118–119

promotions, importance of promoting from within and limiting senior-management-level outside hires, 84–85, 141–142

Q

Qualcomm, 13

R

Reagan, Ronald, 10, 11, 53

recommended readings, 204–205

Reinvent: A Leader's Playbook for Serial Success (Hassan), 47

reputation, importance of being proactive in protecting, 81–82 respect, importance of treating people with, 82

responsibilities, understanding and acceptance of, as personal characteristic of
right people, 136

restructuring actions, importance of being audacious when undertaking, 94–95

results, high, delivering of, as personal characteristic of right people, 135

review of all projects and strategies (proactive action), 48

right people, 127, 131, 133, 136, 138, 142, 147, 148, 152, 153, 194, 199, 200

risk assessment, summary of, 200

risk mitigation, 117–118

risk-mitigation, 49

RJR Nabisco, 29

road map
development of as proactive action, 49–50
for proactive actions, 42

robust sales cadence, backlog, and forecasting system, development of
(proactive action), 56–57

Roosevelt, Theodore, 181

Roper
as example of distinctive culture, 153, 154, 194
as example of highly successful business model recipe, 67–68, 72
as paragon of excellence, 187

RPM, as example of distinctive culture, 153, 154, 194

rules, ten rules for CEOs/leaders to live by, 203

S

Saban, Nick, 101

safety, making of a top priority and core value (proactive action), 55

Sakkab, Nabil, 120

sales cadence
development of process for (proactive action), 56–57
monitoring of, 121

Salvatore Fazzolari Advisors LLC
core values of, 160–161, 197
mission statement, 196

San Jose, Costa Rica, as ideal place for global shared services, 114

scalability, unleashing power of, 96–97

scan, environmental, importance of real-time scan, 121–122

scenarios, importance of analyzing possible ones and preparing for worst, 99

science, investment in, 119–120

self-created enterprise lifelines, 198
self-improvement, continuous (precocious characteristic), 5, 16
self-management, as personal characteristic of right people, 136
self-renewal discipline, of author, 44
self-rescue, importance of, 64
Selingo, Jeffrey J., 97
senior management, promotion from within for, 84–85, 141–142
"Seven Surprises for New CEOs," 54–55
shared global services/global shared services, 12, 70, 89, 110, 114, 190
Shaw, George Bernard, 77
Silverman, Rachel Emma, 141
Simon, William E., 147
Singularity University, mission statement as exemplary, 164, 196
Six-Sigma continuous-improvement discipline, 33, 110, 112, 113, 114–115, 190,
     198
skepticism, pursuit of change with high degree of (proactive action), 53
Southwest Airlines
     as example of company that got recipe right, 66–67
     mission statement as exemplary, 163, 196
speed, importance of, 63
Starbucks, 96
Stern Stewart, 101
Steve Jobs (Isaacson), 6, 47, 66, 70
strategic alliances
     importance of seeking out, 124–125
     as mechanism of learning entity, 79–80
strategic assets, information technology (IT) as, 122–123
Strategic Capitalism: The New Economic Strategy for Winning the Capitalist Cold
     War (D'Aveni), 36, 47
stretch assignments, as indispensable experiences, 25
strong foundation, building of, 132–133
succession-planning process, creation of, 104–105
Sununu, John, 7
supply chain, use of integrated global supply chain, 110, 113–114, 190
surprises for CEOs, 54–55
survival, in business and on the mountain, 64
survival instincts (precocious characteristic), 5, 19
Susquehanna University, author's connections to, 44
sustained leadership, three practices for, overview, 1–2

T

Taleb, Nassim Nicholas, 57, 172
talent management, 25–26
talent-management system
    design of, 110, 120
    innovation in, 140
TE Connectivity, 33
teaching ability (precocious characteristic), 5, 19–20
team playing, as personal characteristic of right people, 135
team-building talents (precocious characteristic), 5, 18
"Technology is the Best Policy," 122
"Tenure at the Top: How Long Is Too Long (or Too Short) for a CEO to Lead a Company?" 40
Thompson Fred, 11
360 review, 58
Tita, Bob, 99
training
    extensive training as indispensable experience, 26
    for new CEOs, 27
transformation and reinvention, lessons learned, 87–97
transformational change, effectively defining, managing, and communicating, 89
transparency (precocious characteristic), 5, 11–12
true economic value, determination of where created (proactive action), 55–56
truthfulness (precocious characteristic), 5, 12
Tuck School of Business (Dartmouth College), 36
Twain, Mark, 9, 12
20 Mile March, 127
Twight, Mark F., 16, 63, 78, 97, 132, 170, 219

U

uncertainty and turbulence, lessons learned, 97–99
Undaunted Courage (Ambrose), 131
Understanding Michael Porter (Magretta), 46
Union Pacific, mission statement as exemplary, 164, 196
University of Pennsylvania Wharton School, 141

V

value selling, taking advantage of, 116–117
Van Gogh, Vincent, xv
variable cost model, implementation of, 117–118
vigilance, importance of, 64

W

Wall Street Journal, 14, 91, 99, 105, 141, 172, 176
Weber, Lauren, 141
Welch, Jack, 15, 19–20, 47, 82, 131, 140–141
Wharton School (University of Pennsylvania), 141
Where Are You on Your Journey from Good to Great? (Collins), 133, 147
Who Says Elephants Can't Dance? (Gerstner), 28, 47
wisdom
 as precocious characteristic, 4, 8
 pursuit of change with (proactive action), 53
Wiseman, Richard, 172, 177
worst, importance of analyzing possible scenarios and preparing for, 99
Wozniak, Stephen, 6

Z

Zemurray, Samuel (Banana Man), 91

Open Book Editions

A Berrett-Koehler Partner

Open Book Editions is a joint venture between Berrett-Koehler Publishers and Author Solutions, the market leader in self-publishing. There are many more aspiring authors who share Berrett-Koehler's mission than we can sustainably publish. To serve these authors, Open Book Editions offers a comprehensive self-publishing opportunity.

A Shared Mission

Open Book Editions welcomes authors who share the Berrett-Koehler mission—Creating a World That Works for All. We believe that to truly create a better world, action is needed at all levels—individual, organizational, and societal. At the individual level, our publications help people align their lives with their values and with their aspirations for a better world. At the organizational level, we promote progressive leadership and management practices, socially responsible approaches to business, and humane and effective organizations. At the societal level, we publish content that advances social and economic justice, shared prosperity, sustainability, and new solutions to national and global issues.

Open Book Editions represents a new way to further the BK mission and expand our community. We look forward to helping more authors challenge conventional thinking, introduce new ideas, and foster positive change.

For more information, see the Open Book Editions website: http://www.iuniverse.com/Packages/OpenBookEditions.aspx

Join the BK Community! See exclusive author videos, join discussion groups, find out about upcoming events, read author blogs, and much more! http://bkcommunity.com/